Rome

Select

contents

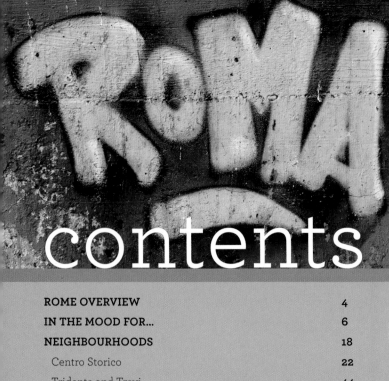

Rome overview

From hub of an empire to Papal headquarters, Romans have long considered their home to be Caput Mundi, capital of the world. While Rome's influence may not be as global as it once was, the evident attractions of the city that have brought travellers for centuries remain as they always have been. It has incomparable art and architecture, lively and generous people, exciting cuisine and world-beating coffee and *gelato*. But the 21st century has brought a breath of fresh air to this ancient city.

The millennial revamp for Holy Year 2000, which gave the city's ancient sites a much-needed facelift, sparked a revolution in the dormant artistic and architectural scenes, and Rome has seen a swathe of renovations and openings. The most radical of these is MAXXI, a recently inaugurated grand project by British-Iraqi architect Zaha Hadid, which sees a former army barracks reborn as the Museum of 21st-Century Arts. There's also Richard Meier's light-filled pavilion for the Ara Pacis, an ancient

Roman altar, and the Centrale Montemartini museum, an imaginatively converted power plant in Ostiense that houses part of the Capitoline Museums' vast collection of ancient statuary. Rome's dynamic arts scene includes one of the most vibrant music venues in Italy, Renzo Piano's Parco della Musica, where beetle-like pods create perfect acoustics in settings suitable for symphonies or soul. While not exactly a new Dolce Vita, there is a cinematic gloss to the contemporary city: a funky club scene, sleek cafés, boutique hotels, eclectic festivals, and a more cosmopolitan air.

Days and evenings are to be enjoyed to the fullest. At any given moment, you will find cafés, bars, restaurants and squares buzzing with life. Romans are fearless and they expect you to be as well – whether zipping around on a Vespa or indulging in the local *quinto quarto* cuisine.

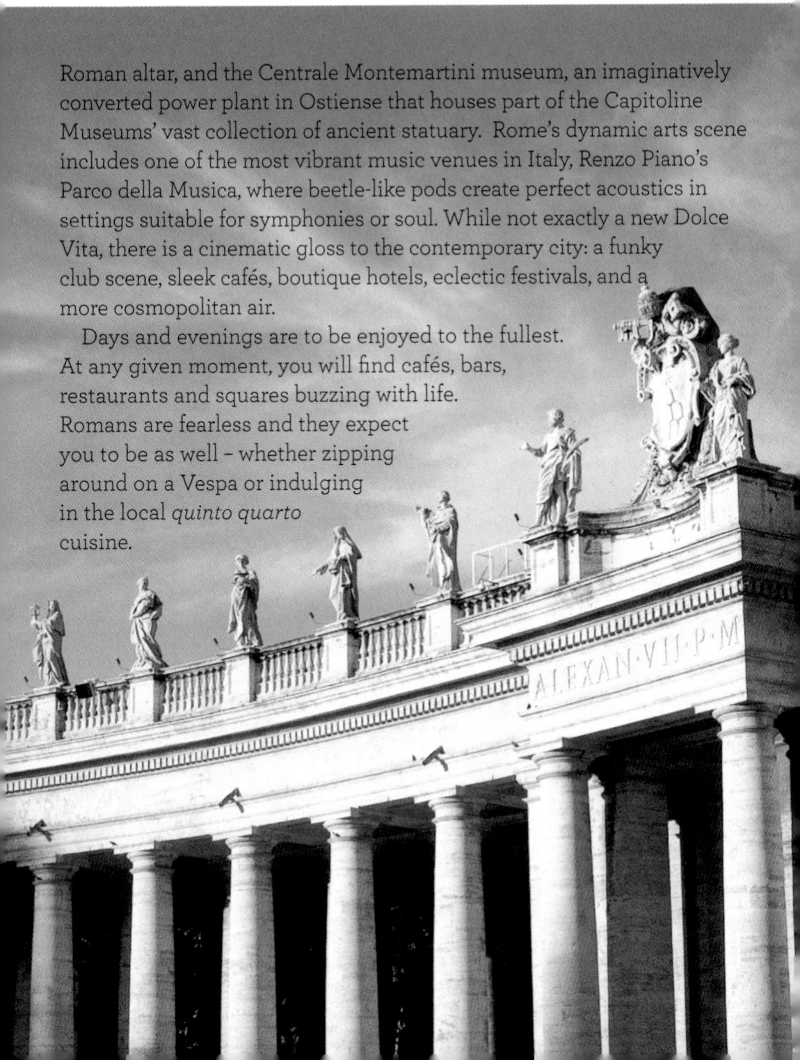

in the mood for...

... romance

As many a Roman will proudly point out, the name of their great city is *Amor* spelt backwards. Roma certainly qualifies as one of the world's most romantic travel destinations. This is where English **Romantic poets** *(p.160)* expired, and where love and life are affirmed on the back of a **Vespa** *(p.143), alla Roman Holiday*. For unforgettable moments, toast the sunburnt cityscape from the rooftop of the **St George Hotel** *(p.35)* or lose yourself in an evening stroll around **Piazza Navona** *(p.42)*. Lovebirds looking for a moment away from the chaos should pack some Prosecco for an afternoon at the **Giardino degli Aranci** *(p.158)*. If money is no object, spend a weekend in imperial opulence at the **Residenza Napoleon III** *(p.173)* or be pampered together at the **Kami Spa** *(p.58)*. Whatever the wallet weighs, the diehard romantic should plan on proposing at the **Trevi Fountain** *(p.59)* when all it takes is one small coin to ensure true love.

... fine dining

The true gourmand knows that a getaway in Rome means a reservation at **La Pergola**, Rome's only Michelin 3-star restaurant *(p.75; pictured above right)*, with creative haute cuisine and a spectacular view over the city. For a more traditional Roman gourmet experience, sit in the front row of Piazza del Popolo at **Dal Bolognese** *(p.61)*, where Italian glitterati show off their best looks while dining on superb Emiliana-Romagnola cuisine. A relative newcomer to the dining scene is **Open Colonna**, the Palazzo delle Esposizioni's rooftop restaurant *(p.149)* and the latest one-star Michelin restaurant – here's where the foodies come for brunch. Throwing down the nouvelle cuisine gauntlet is the recently reopened **Casina Valadier** *(p.127)*, perched on the Pincio hill – a spectacular view and even more spectacular menu. Get to the bottom of the wonderful wine cellar in **Checchino dal 1887** and eat like the Pope in **Cantina Tirolese** *(p.71)*, Benedict XVI's favourite fondue restaurant.

... ancient history

Rome is the world's most beautiful walking museum. For centuries people have been visiting to see for themselves what the fuss is all about. You'll soon find out with a stroll through the **Roman Forum** *(p.86, pictured)*, where Mark Antony made his speech after Caesar's assassination, or stand beneath the dome of the **Pantheon** *(p.26)* and be illuminated in a way you never have before, while the **Colosseum** *(p.95)* looks so much more impressive in reality than on postcards. Another place to head for a sense of the grandeur of ancient Rome is the recently reopened hall at the **Baths of Diocletian** *(p.147)*. If you have time, be sure to include a visit to the **church of San Clemente** *(p.94)* to see the underground temple to Mithras, and the **Case Romane** *(p.98)* where you can see classical literature performed. Then put it all into perspective at EUR's **Museum of Roman Civilisation** *(p.168)* where there's a fantastic detailed model of ancient Rome.

... local flavour

When in Rome, everyone wants to feel like a local, and there's no better way to do so than by sampling the cooking. The fearless gastronome will head to **Testaccio** *(p.162)* and delve into the *quinto quarto* for an experience in offal, while epicureans will ponder the secret to the perfect *carbonara* at **Da Carlone** *(p.117)*. Head to the **Ghetto** for Jewish delicacies *(p.40)* like delicious fried artichokes. For a fix of local street food, try *suppli* (fried rice balls) in **Trastevere** *(p.110)*, and then grab a refreshing *grattachecca* at **Sora Mirella** *(p.104)*.

... staying out late

Rome is a great place for late-night adventures. Head away from the historic centre to **Testaccio** for dancing and clubbing *(p.166)*. If bar hopping is more your style, atmospheric **Trastevere** will suit you best *(p.107)*, and though the **Via Veneto** isn't the celebrity and paparazzi hangout it once was, you might want to see where *La Dolce Vita* began. In summertime head for the river and the **Ponte Milvio** bars *(p.78)*, while **Campo de' Fiori** *(p.41)* amasses the study-abroad crowd until the police send them home.

... modern and contemporary art and architecture

Finally Rome is blossoming in the contemporary art scene. Take a quick history lesson in modern Italian art at the **National Gallery for Modern and Contemporary Art** *(p.130)*, where you can learn about the Futurists. A visit to Zaha Hadid's dynamic **MAXXI** *(p.134; pictured)* will give you a better idea of contemporary artists and architects working in Italy. And Richard Meier's cutting-edge glass-and-travertine building adds a terrific twist to the ancient **Ara Pacis** *(p.49)*.

... being pampered

Ancient Romans invented the art of indulgence – the city once had more than 600 baths. Present-day Rome keeps up the tradition with lavish spas to rejuvenate you after all the sightseeing. **Wonderfool** dedicates its services to a gentlemen-only clientele *(p.36)*, though women do sneak in on Tuesdays. **Acqua Madre's** women-only weekdays are set in a bathhouse-style atmosphere *(p.37)*. For supreme spoiling, soak yourself in the marble and bronze baths at the Grand Spa at the **Cavalieri Hilton** *(p.173)*.

... wine tasting

From simple wine bars to flashy academies, there is always somewhere just around the corner for the novice taster and the knowledgeable nose. The local *enoteca* (wine bar) is every neighbourhood's prize, and the Centro Storico leads the way with two of the most charming and best-stocked wine bars, **Il Goccetto** and **Angolo Divino** *(p.32)*, which serve delicious antipasti along with the wines. **Novecento** *(p.33)*, a no-frills wine bar, is the place to wait for your dinner reservations while sipping on some Barolo.

Tridente's posh **Il Palazzetto** *(p.52)* is home to the prestigious Wine Academy with courses for serious sommeliers wishing to perfect their palates. For an elegant tasting of Italy's best, **Casa Bleve** will not disappoint *(p.32)*. Or head to Trastevere – **Enoteca Ferrara** will delight not only with its labels but also with its social scene *(p.107)*.

... Renaissance and Baroque art

From the Renaissance to the Baroque, for three centuries paintings, sculpture and architecture shaped the city. The star performer is the **Vatican Museums** *(p.72)*, a vast repository of art touched by the masterful hand of Michelangelo. Two great rivals, Bernini and Borromini were the masters of Roman Baroque, pioneering sublime and spectacular effects. Visit their **churches on Via del Quirinale** *(p.148)* and judge for yourself who was best.

But to truly enjoy Rome's Renaissance and Baroque art, you have to visit the smaller galleries like **Villa Farnesina** *(p.114)*, with its loggia of Raphael frescoes, or **Palazzo Corsini** *(p.112)* across the street. The jewels in Rome's Baroque and Renaissance crown are **Galleria Borghese** *(p.126)* for its amazing collection of Bernini and Caravaggio masterpieces and the exclusive **Palazzo Colonna** *(p.54)*. Runners-ups are the **Galleria Doria Pamphilj** *(p.54)* and the bombastic **Palazzo Barberini** *(p.133)*.

... a coffee break

Coffee connoisseurs should elbow their way to the bar of **Sant'Eustachio** or **Tazza D'Oro** – quintessential Roman caffès and longstanding rivals for the perfect coffee *(p.28)*. For a leisurely caffeine fix or freshly squeezed orange juice on a tranquil square, head to **Caffè Farnese** *(p.38)*. Too early? Go for brunch at stylish **Ciampini** *(p.48)*. Or head for the former studio of neoclassical sculptor **Canova** *(p.60)*, and have a cappuccino among the casts.

... an inspirational view

This beautiful city with its terracotta rooftops and countless cupolas is meant to be admired from above. The dome of **St Peter's** *(p.74)* itself is an excellent vantage point *(view pictured)*, but the all-time favourite look-out spots are the **Fontanone** *(p.108)* on the Gianicolo, and nearby **Piazzale Garibaldi** *(p.113)*. If taking in an exhibition at the **Scuderie**, be sure to stop at the Great Window *(p.141)* for a view. Drink in more wonderful views and some welcome refreshment from the top of the **Vittoriano Monument** *(p.88)*. Or enjoy a sunset view over the domes and rootftops from the 5th-floor terrace of **Il Palazzetto** *(p.52)*.

... retail therapy

Whether you are a pilgrim on a budget or a well-heeled globetrotter with a platinum Amex card, shopping in Rome is always fun. The city's window-dressers have a flair for transforming displays into artistic still-lifes, so even window-shopping becomes a rewarding retail experience. The honeypot for fashionistas is the busy intersection of **Via dei Condotti** and **Via del Corso** *(p.56–7)*, though shopping in Rome isn't limited to the Tridente area.

More affordable **Monti** *(p.144)* has established itself as the centre for alternative designers' and vintage shops, particularly in the winding streets between Via dei Serpenti and Via Urbana. And **Via dei Coronari** *(p.30)* above Piazza Navona is lined with antiques dealers and one-of-a-kind boutiques.

For gourmet treats visit **Franchi Gastronomia** *(p.80)* - gift baskets of its wines, oils, meats and cheeses can be shipped abroad. **Volpetti** *(p.163)* can also vacuum-pack their finest meats and cheeses for you.

And don't forget the museum and gallery shops: the **Vatican Museums** *(p.72)* shop is a great source for gifts and mementoes while the bookstore at the **Scuderie** *(p.141)* stocks excellent art books.

... a breath of fresh air

Rome may be an open-air museum, but it is also a den of traffic-clogged streets with pedestrians, scooters, buses and cars jostling for space. If you need to take a break from the hubbub there are plenty of options nearby. Head to **Villa Borghese**, for example, for a rural stroll or some rollerblading *(p.124)*, or a take a morning bike ride down Rome's oldest road, **Via Appia Antica** *(p.97; pictured)*. For those who prefer to stay citybound, rent a bike for a trip by the **Tiber** *(p.78)* in the afternoon or enjoy an amble around the **Botanical Gardens**, hidden in Trastevere *(p.112)*, or enjoy a more formal tour of the **Vatican Gardens** *(p.77)*.

There are plenty of places for a picnic: pack up your deli or market produce and head to the **Palatine hill** *(p.90)* or over to the **Circus Maximus** for an afternoon sunbathe *(p.99)*. To get lungs full of fresh air while sticking with the crowds, go and shout for a football or rugby team at the **Olympic Stadium** or **Stadio Flaminio** *(p.128)*. For a couple of hours out of town altogether, head for **Ostia Antica** *(p.169)*; it's just 4km from Lido di Ostia and the beach.

... family fun

Parents will soon discover that no matter where you go, Romans love children. But finding things to do with kids, big and small, seems daunting in a city not adapted for the trappings of the modern parent. Though Rome's cobblestones and narrow pavements aren't designed for power pushchairs and prams, the parks are. Head to Villa Borghese's **Casina di Raffaello** *(p.124)*, an indoor/outdoor children's area, or set yourself free in the park for rollerblading, bike riding, theatres and a century-old zoo. Across town the **Gianicolo** hill *(p.113)* has an 18th-century puppet show with daily performances, pony rides and a noon-time cannon. Indoor entertainment with history attached isn't hard to find – **RomeRewind** *(p.95)* re-creates gladiatorial combat in a 3-D movie. For something less intensive, head to **Da Meo Patacca** *(p.115)*, a 19th-century themed restaurant, where waiters serve Roman cuisine and culture in period costumes. But wherever you are, there's always ice cream to uplift the spirits...

... gelato

The perfect *gelato* is a much debated subject in Rome. Flavour, quality and atmosphere are the three main requirements. Exquisite chocolate and pistachio are found at **Gelateria al Teatro** *(p.30)*, a small *gelateria* tucked into an alley behind Piazza Navona. The vast choice and unique flavours of **Giolitti** *(p.65)* have a wide following, hence the queues. Brunch spot **Ciampini** *(p.48)* has a hidden *gelateria* in the back bar that should not be overlooked.

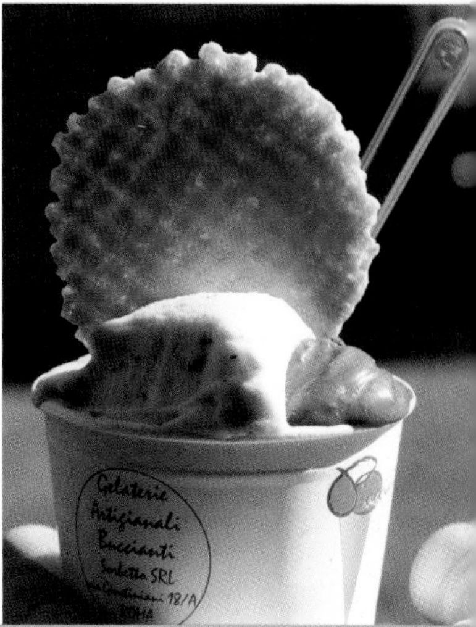

... music

Rome has some of the most beautiful music venues in the world. Renzo Piano's modern masterpiece **Auditorium** *(p.135; pictured)* is the atmospheric centre of Rome's music scene. Take in some opera under the stars at the **Baths of Caracalla** *(p.139)* or at the more traditional **Teatro dell'Opera** *(p.151)*. The **Quirinale Palace** hosts chamber concerts twice a month *(p.140)*, and the **Theatre of Marcellus** *(p.96)* is a scenic backdrop for a lively summer festival.

neighbourhoods

Originally, Rome was founded on the famous Seven Hills that sit on the eastern bank of the serpentine River Tiber. The hills of the Aventine, Capitoline, Caelian, Esquiline, Palatine, Quirinale and Viminale have been inhabited since at least 1,000 BC. These areas still form the core of the city centre, but over the ages Rome has expanded to include the Villa Borghese park to the north, and Trastevere and Prati across the river.

Centro Storico Rome's historic centre is the heart of city and country. Italy's parliament and senate are set among hotels, restaurants, schools and businesses. The most beautiful piazzas – Navona, Rotonda, Farnese and Campo de' Fiori – are here, but the true beauty is in the side streets where ancient and medieval architectural details constantly surprise.

Tridente and Trevi Tridente is the Centro Storico's smart next-door neighbour. Starting from Piazza del Popolo, Tridente's central prong travels the length of the 1.5km-long Via del Corso, while Via Ripetta extends towards the Ara Pacis and boutique-lined Via del Babuino leads to the Spanish Steps. At the very edge of Tridente, off another favourite shopping street, Via del Tritone, is the Trevi Fountain.

The Vatican, Borgo and Prati Vatican City, the centre of the Catholic world, lies between the medieval pilgrims' quarter of the Borgo and residential Prati. Here visitors flock to see St Peter's Basilica and the Vatican Museums, or join an audience with the Pope. Prati means meadows, but the gardens and vineyards have long been built over, and today it is known for food markets and boutiques.

Colosseo and Celio The enclave from Piazza Venezia to the Celio hill contains Rome's most ancient and archetypical sites, including the Roman Forum and Colosseum. Less known is the quiet neighbourhood behind the Colosseum – Celio – where ancient Roman houses lie beneath medieval churches.

Trastevere and the Gianicolo Trastevere considers itself a country within a city, as the local community, the Trasteverini, have lived here for centuries, eschewing change. Though it has gentrified over the last few decades, the neighbourhood is still postcard perfect and a preferred evening hang-out. Towering above, the Gianicolo hill is a quiet residential area, boasting the best view of Rome.

Villa Borghese, Via Veneto and Flaminia Via Veneto achieved international celebrity with Fellini's 1960 film *La Dolce Vita*, a title ever associated with this street of chic cafés. Now the embassy and luxury hotel district, Via Veneto is also a gateway to the gardens of Villa Borghese and the valley beyond where Rome's sporting arenas and new contemporary art centre are located.

Quirinale, Repubblica and Esquilino The hills and valleys of the Quirinale and Esquilino contain Rome's greatest social contrasts. On the Quirinale is the home of Italy's President, while in the valley beneath, the 'it' neighbourhood of Monti reigns as *the* original working-class neighbourhood and hipster hang-out. The business district from Via Nazionale to Piazza della Repubblica is picking up speed with the new Palazzo delle Esposizioni exhibition gallery and rooftop restaurant.

Aventino, Testaccio and Piramide Aventino is the quiet and prestigious neighbourhood overlooking the Circus Maximus. Round the other side, Aventino flows down to Testaccio, an old warehouse district and centre of Rome's nightlife, where music of every kind is represented at its many clubs. Looming behind busy Testaccio is the Piramide, Rome's quirky 1st-century tomb, which designates city limits and newer neighbourhoods.

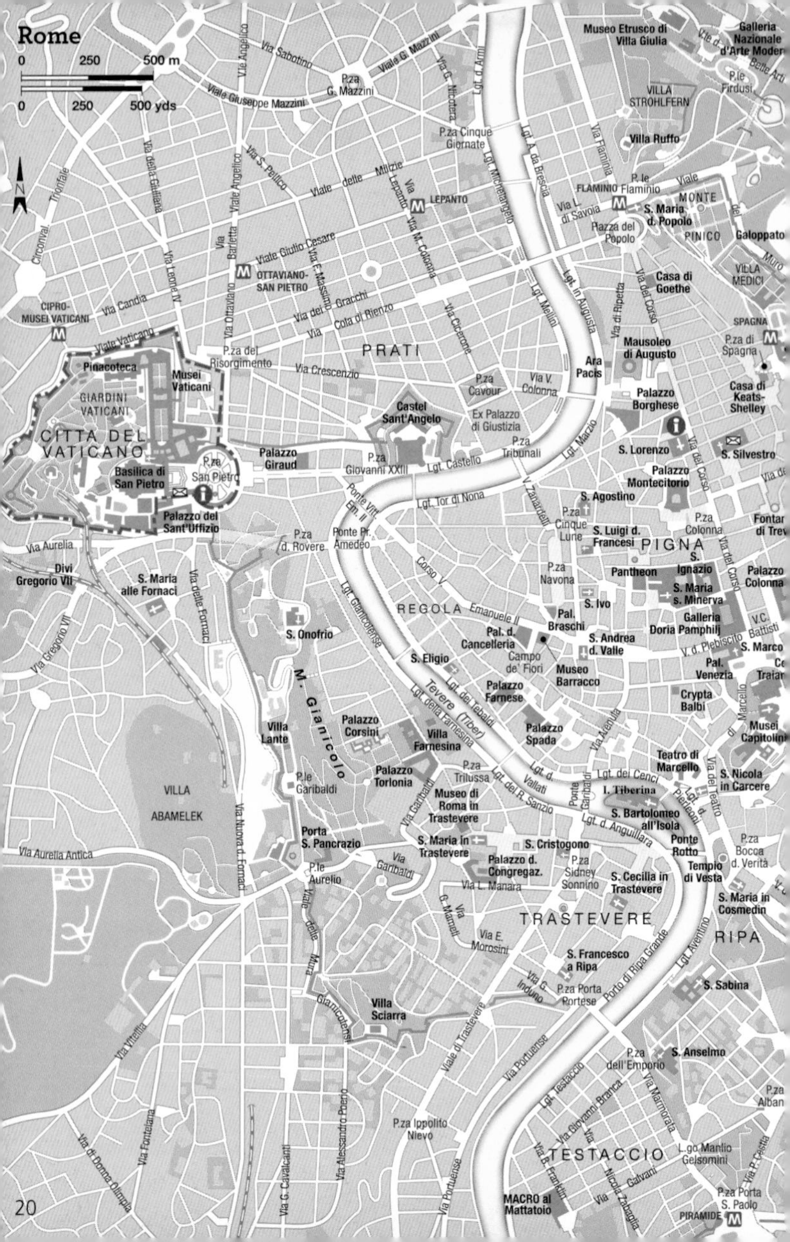
Rome
0 250 500 m
0 250 500 yds
N
Museo Etrusco di Villa Giulia
Galleria Nazionale d'Arte Moderna
Belle Arti
P.le Firdusi
VILLA STROHLFERN
Villa Ruffo
Via Sabotino
Viale G. Mazzini
P.za G. Mazzini
Viale Giuseppe Mazzini
V.le Angelico
Via G. Nicotera
Lgt. d. Armi
P.za Cinque Giornate
Lgt. A. da Brescia
Lgt. Michelangelo
Via Flaminia
FLAMINIO
P.le Flaminio
Viale
MONTE
S. Maria d. Popolo
Via L. di Savoia
Piazza del Popolo
PINCIO
Galoppatoio
Muro
VILLA MEDICI
Via della Giuliana
Via S. Pellico
Viale Angelico
Viale delle Milizie
Via Lepanto
LEPANTO
Via M. Colonna
Trionfale
Circonval.
Via Barletta
Via Leone IV
Via Ottaviano
Viale Giulio Cesare
OTTAVIANO-SAN PIETRO
Via F. Massimi
Via dei Gracchi
Via Cola di Rienzo
Lgt. Mellini
Lgt. in Augusta
Via di Ripetta
Via del Corso
Casa di Goethe
CIPRO-MUSEI VATICANI
Via Candia
Viale Vaticano
SPAGNA
P.za di Spagna
Via Cicerone
PRATI
P.za del Risorgimento
Via Crescenzio
Mausoleo di Augusto
Ara Pacis
Pinacoteca
Musei Vaticani
GIARDINI VATICANI
P.za Cavour
Via V. Colonna
Palazzo Borghese
Casa di Keats-Shelley
Castel Sant'Angelo
Ex Palazzo di Giustizia
Lgt. Marzio
CITTA DEL VATICANO
P.za San Pietro
Basilica di San Pietro
Palazzo Giraud
P.za Giovanni XXIII
Lgt. Castello
P.za Tribunali
S. Lorenzo
S. Silvestro
Palazzo Montecitorio
Via del Corso
Via del
Palazzo del Sant'Uffizio
Ponte Vitt. Em. II
Lgt. Tor di Nona
V. Zanardelli
S. Agostino
P.za Cinque Lune
S. Luigi d. Francesi
P.za Colonna
Fontana di Trevi
Via Aurelia
P.za d. Rovere
Ponte Pr. Amedeo
PIGNA
Divi
Gregorio VII
S. Maria alle Fornaci
Via delle Fornaci
Corso V. Emanuele II
P.za Navona
Pantheon
S. Ignazio
Palazzo Colonna
S. Maria s. Minerva
S. Ivo
Lgt. Gianicolense
REGOLA
Pal. Braschi
Galleria Doria Pamphilj
V.C. Battisti
Via Gregorio VII
S. Onofrio
Pal. d. Cancelleria
S. Andrea d. Valle
V. d. Plebiscito
S. Marco
Campo de' Fiori
Museo Barracco
S. Eligio
Pal. Venezia
Traiano
M. Gianicolo
Lgt. dei Tebaldi
Tevere (Tiber)
Lgt. della Farnesina
Palazzo Farnese
Crypta Balbi
Via Arenula
Palazzo Spada
Palazzo Corsini
Villa Farnesina
Villa Lante
Via d. Marcello
Musei Capitolini
VILLA ABAMELEK
P.le Garibaldi
Palazzo Torlonia
P.za Trilussa
Lgt. d. Vallati
Teatro di Marcello
Via del Teatro
S. Nicola in Carcere
Lgt. dei Cenci
I. Tiberina
Ponte Garibaldi
Lgt. del R. Sanzio
Via Garibaldi
Museo di Roma in Trastevere
Lgt. d. Pierleoni
S. Bartolomeo all'Isola
Lgt. d. Anguillara
Via Nuova d. Fornaci
Porta S. Pancrazio
S. Maria in Trastevere
S. Cristogono
Ponte Rotto
P.za Bocca d. Verità
Via Aurelia Antica
P.le Aurelio
Via Garibaldi
Palazzo d. Congregaz.
P.za Sidney Sonnino
S. Cecilia in Trastevere
Tempio di Vesta
Via L. Manara
S. Maria in Cosmedin
Viale delle Mura
Via G. Mameli
TRASTEVERE
RIPA
Via E. Morosini
S. Francesco a Ripa
Lgt. Aventino
Via G. Induno
P.za Porta Portese
Porto di Ripa Grande
S. Sabina
Gianicolense
Villa Sciarra
Viale di Trastevere
Via Vitellia
Via Portuense
P.za dell'Emporio
S. Anselmo
Lgt. Testaccio
Via Giovanni Branca
Via Marmorata
P.za Albania
Via Fonteiana
Via di Donna Olimpia
Via G. Cavalcanti
Via Alessandro Poerio
P.za Ippolito Nievo
Via Portuense
TESTACCIO
L.go Manlio Gelsomini
Via B. Franklin
Via Galvani
Via Nicola Zabaglia
Via P. Cestia
P.za Porta S. Paolo
MACRO al Mattatoio
PIRAMIDE

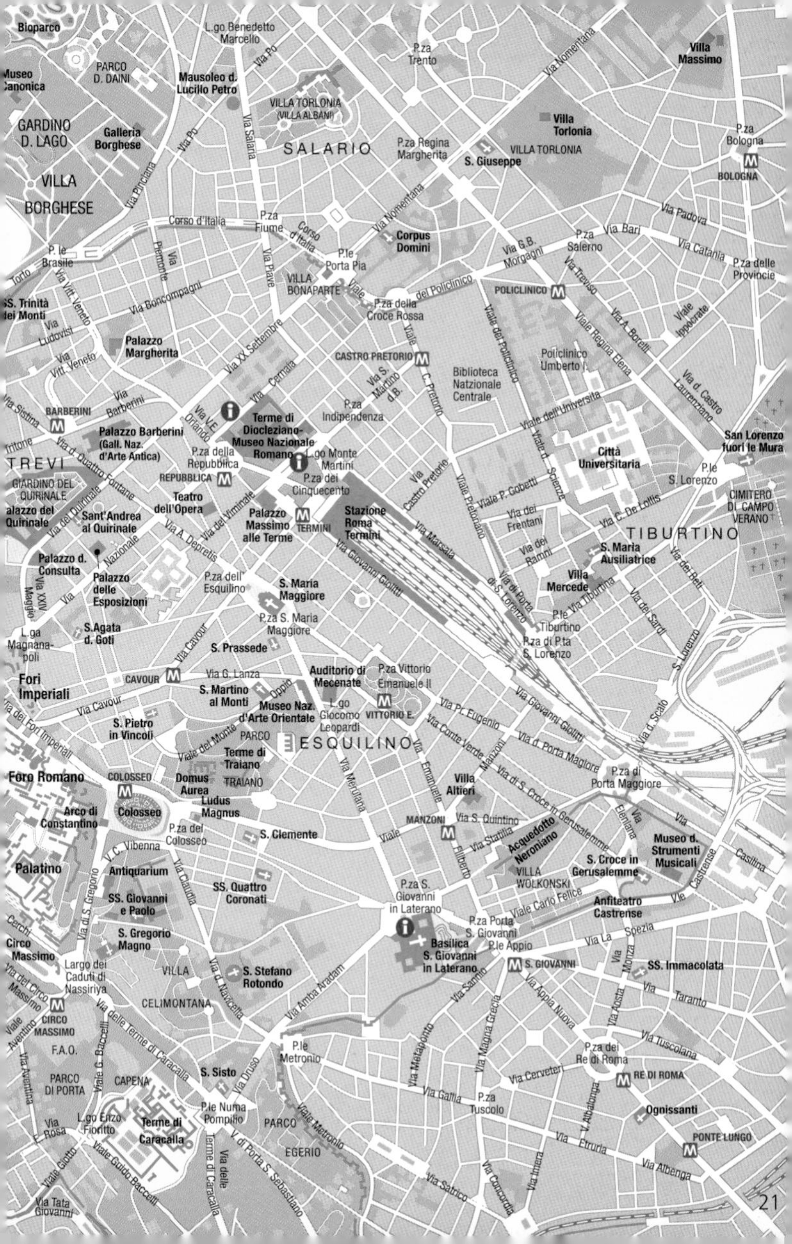
Bioparco
L.go Benedetto Marcello
Museo Canonica
PARCO D. DAINI
Mausoleo d. Lucilio Petro
VILLA TORLONIA (VILLA ALBANI)
P.za Trento
Via Nomentana
Villa Massimo
GARDINO D. LAGO
Galleria Borghese
Via Po
Via Salaria
SALARIO
P.za Regina Margherita
Villa Torlonia
VILLA TORLONIA
S. Giuseppe
P.za Bologna
BOLOGNA
VILLA BORGHESE
Via Pinciana
Corso d'Italia
P.za Fiume
Via Padova
P.za Salerno
Via Bari
Via Catania
P.za delle Provincie
P.le Brasile
Via Piemonte
Via Piave
P.le Porta Pia
Corpus Domini
Via G.B. Morgagni
SS. Trinità dei Monti
Via Vitt. Veneto
Via Boncompagni
VILLA BONAPARTE
P.za della Croce Rossa
Viale del Policlinico
POLICLINICO
Via Treviso
Viale Ippocrate
Via Ludovisi
Palazzo Margherita
Via XX Settembre
CASTRO PRETORIO
Policlinico Umberto I
Viale Regina Elena
Via A. Borelli
Via Cernaia
Via S. Martino d.B.
Biblioteca Natzionale Centrale
Via d. Castro Laurenziano
Via Sistina
BARBERINI
Via Barberini
P.za Indipendenza
Viale dell'Università
Via V.E. Orlando
Terme di Diocleziano-Museo Nazionale Romano
Palazzo Barberini (Gall. Naz. d'Arte Antica)
L.go Monte Martini
Città Universitaria
San Lorenzo fuori le Mura
TREVI
P.za della Repubblica
P.za dei Cinquecento
P.le S. Lorenzo
GIARDINO DEL QUIRINALE
REPUBBLICA
Teatro dell'Opera
Via Castro Pretorio
Viale P. Gobetti
CIMITERO DI CAMPO VERANO
Palazzo del Quirinale
Sant'Andrea al Quirinale
Via Nazionale
Palazzo Massimo alle Terme
TERMINI
Stazione Roma Termini
Via dei Frentani
Via C. De Lollis
TIBURTINO
Via A. Depretis
Via del Viminale
Via Marsala
Via dei Ramni
S. Maria Ausiliatrice
Palazzo d. Consulta
Palazzo delle Esposizioni
P.za dell' Esquilino
S. Maria Maggiore
Via Giovanni Giolitti
Villa Mercede
Via Tiburtina
Via dei Reti
Via dei Sardi
P.za S. Maria Maggiore
P.le Tiburtino
S.Agata d. Goti
Via Cavour
L.ga Magnanapoli
S. Prassede
P.za di P.ta S. Lorenzo
Fori Imperiali
CAVOUR
Via G. Lanza
Auditorio di Mecenate
P.za Vittorio Emanuele II
S. Martino al Monti
Museo Naz. d'Arte Orientale
L.go Giocomo Leopardi
VITTORIO E.
Via Pr. Eugenio
Via d. Scalo
Via dei Fori Imperiali
S. Pietro in Vincoli
PARCO
ESQUILINO
Via Conte Verde
Via d. Porta Maggiore
Terme di Traiano
Via Merulana
Via Emanuele
Foro Romano
COLOSSEO
Domus Aurea
TRAIANO
Villa Altieri
Via di S. Croce in Gerusalemme
P.za di Porta Maggiore
Ludus Magnus
Arco di Constantino
Colosseo
P.za del Colosseo
MANZONI
Via S. Quintino
S. Clemente
Via Stabilia
Acquedotto Neroniano
Museo d. Strumenti Musicali
Via Casilina
V. C. Vibenna
Via Claudia
Palatino
Antiquarium
S. Croce in Gerusalemme
VILLA WOLKONSKI
SS. Quattro Coronati
P.za S. Giovanni in Laterano
SS. Giovanni e Paolo
Viale Carlo Felice
Anfiteatro Castrense
P.za Porta S. Giovanni
S. Gregorio Magno
Basilica S. Giovanni in Laterano
P.le Appio
Via La Spezia
Circo Massimo
S. GIOVANNI
SS. Immacolata
Largo dei Caduti di Nassiriya
VILLA
S. Stefano Rotondo
Via Taranto
Via Amba Aradam
CELIMONTANA
Via Appia Nuova
Via Aosta
Via Tuscolana
CIRCO MASSIMO
F.A.O.
P.le Metronio
P.za dei Re di Roma
Via Cerveteri
RE DI ROMA
PARCO DI PORTA
CAPENA
S. Sisto
Via Druso
Via Metaponto
Via Magna Grecia
P.le Numa Pompilio
Via Gallia
P.za Tuscolo
Ognissanti
Via Rosa
L.go Enzo Fioritto
Terme di Caracalla
PARCO EGERIO
Viale Metronio
Via Etruria
PONTE LUNGO
Viale Giotto
Viale Guido Baccelli
Via delle Terme di Caracalla
V. di Porta S. Sebastiano
Via Satrico
Via Concordia
Via Albenga
Via Tata Giovanni

M·AGRIPPA

Centro Storico

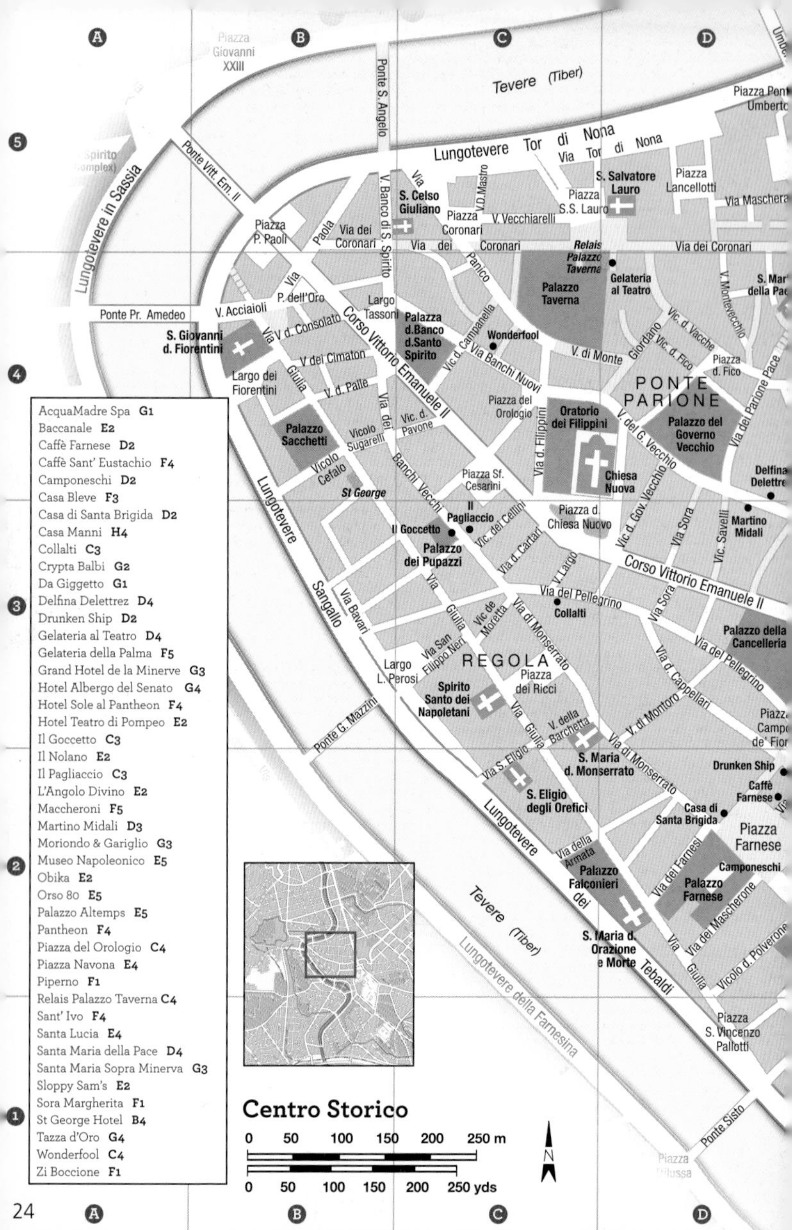

Centro Storico

AcquaMadre Spa **G1**
Baccanale **E2**
Caffè Farnese **D2**
Caffè Sant' Eustachio **F4**
Camponeschi **D2**
Casa Bleve **F3**
Casa di Santa Brigida **D2**
Casa Manni **H4**
Collalti **C3**
Crypta Balbi **G2**
Da Giggetto **G1**
Delfina Delettrez **D4**
Drunken Ship **D2**
Gelateria al Teatro **D4**
Gelateria della Palma **F5**
Grand Hotel de la Minerve **G3**
Hotel Albergo del Senato **G4**
Hotel Sole al Pantheon **F4**
Hotel Teatro di Pompeo **E2**
Il Goccetto **C3**
Il Nolano **E2**
Il Pagliaccio **C3**
L'Angolo Divino **E2**
Maccheroni **F5**
Martino Midali **D3**
Moriondo & Gariglio **G3**
Museo Napoleonico **E5**
Obika **E2**
Orso 80 **E5**
Palazzo Altemps **E5**
Pantheon **F4**
Piazza del Orologio **C4**
Piazza Navona **E4**
Piperno **F1**
Relais Palazzo Taverna **C4**
Sant' Ivo **F4**
Santa Lucia **E4**
Santa Maria della Pace **D4**
Santa Maria Sopra Minerva **G3**
Sloppy Sam's **E2**
Sora Margherita **F1**
St George Hotel **B4**
Tazza d'Oro **G4**
Wonderfool **C4**
Zi Boccione **F1**

E
F
G
H
S. Antonio d. Portoghesi
Orso 80
Via dell' Orso
Via d. Portoghesi
Via della Scrofa
Via dei Prefetti
Piazza Firenze
Via Valdina
Piazza del Parlamento
Palazzo Ruspoli
Via dei Soldati
V. d. Gigli d'Oro
Via dei Pianellari
V. d. Stelletta
Piazza in Campo Marzio
Via d. C. Marzio
Via d. Missione
Camera dei Deputati
V. Dell' Impresa
Palazzo Chigi
V. del Tritone
Galleria Alberto Sordi
Zanardelli
Palazzo Altemps
S. Apollinare
P.za S. Apollinare
S. Agostino
Piazza S. Agostino
V. Spagnoli
Piazza delle Coppelle
S. Maria
Via Uffici d. Vicario
Palazzo di Montecitorio
Piazza Colonna
Via del Corso
Maccheroni
Via della Maddalena
Gelateria della Palma
Piazza di Montecitorio
Via d. Coppelle
Piazza Cinque Lune
V. Colonna Antonina
Casa Manni
Santa Lucia
Largo Febo
Via P. d. Cornacchie
Piazza Maddalena
Via in Aquiro
Piazza Capranica
Piazza di Pietra
V. di Pietra
S. Luigi d. Francesi
Corso del Rinascimento
Hotel Sole al Pantheon
Tazza d'Oro
Via del Pastini
Palazzo d. Borsa
Via Montecatini
Maria Anima
Piazza Navona
V. Salvatore
Via Giustiniani
Piazza d. Rotonda
Hotel Albergo del Senato
Piazza Santa Ignazio
V. Caravita
Via di Snta Marina dell' Anima
Palazzo Madama (Senato)
S. Eustachio
Via Seminario
V. d. Collegio Romano
S. Marcello
S. Agnese in Agone
Pantheon
Via d. Minerva
Santa Ignazio
Via d. Ignazio
Piazza S. Eustachio
Palazzo della Sapienza
S. Ivo
Caffè Sant Eustachio
Via Rotonda
Santa Maria Sopra Minerva
Palazzo Doria Pamphilj
V. d. Sediari
Piazza Minerva
Moriondo & Gariglio
Piazza Collegio Romano
S. Maria v. Lata
Palazzo Braschi (Museo di Roma)
Via dei Teatro Valle
Casa Bleve
Via Monterone
Via S. Catherina s. Siena
V. d. Pie' di Marmo
Teatro Valle
Grand Hotel de la Minerve
S. Pantaleo
Piazza d. S. Pantaleo
Palazzo Massimo
Piazza d. Pigna
S. Stefano
V. d. Gatta
Galleria Doria Pamphilj
Palazzo Bonaparte
Via A. d. Ciambella
V. d. Cestari
Piazza Grazioli
Museo Barracco (Palazzo d. Piccola Farnesina)
Piazza S. Andrea della Valle
SS Stimmate d. San Francisco
Via del Gesù
Palazzo Altieri
Argentina
Corso Vittorio
V. d. Plebiscito
Piazza Venezia
S. Andrea d. Valle
P.za dei Paradiso
Palazzo Vidoni
Largo di Torre Argentina
Baullari
Via dei Sudario
Corso V. Emanuele II
Palazzo Venezia
S. Marco
Baccanale
P.za dei Biscione
Hotel Teatro di Pompeo
Teatro Argentina
Area Sacra
V. S. Nicola de Cesarini
V. Arco d. Ginnasi
Piazza del Gesù
Chiesa del Gesù
Astalli
Piazza S. Marco
Nolano
Sloppy Sam's
Via dei Barbieri
Via Torre
Via S. Marco
L'Angolo Divino
Teatro di Pompeo
Via d. Monte della Farina
Via delle Botteghe Oscure
Crypta Balbi
S. Stanislao
Via d'Aracoeli
Via Santa Anna
Largo Arenula
Via dei Giubbonari
V. Paganica
V. Caetani
Via d. Polacchi
S. Carlo ai Catinari
S. ANGELO
Palazzo Mattei
S. Caterina
Piazza d' Aracoeli
Piazza del Monte di Pietà
Via dei Falegnami
Via dei Funari
Via del Delfini
V. di or de' Soecchi
Palazzo d. Monte di Pietà
Piazza Costaguti
Piazza Mattei
Via del Teatro di Marcello
Via dei Specchi
Piazza Cairoli
V. Pianto
Piazza Capizzucchi
S.S. Trinità d. Pellegrini
Sora Margherita
Zi Boccione
AcquaMadre Spa
S. Ambrogio Massima
S. Maria in Monticelli
Arenula
S. Maria del Pianto
Via Portico d' Ottavia
S. Maria Campitelli
S. Paolo alle Regola
Piazza Cinque Scole
Da Giggetto
Palazzo Cenci
S. Angelo in Pescheria
V. Conservatorio
Piazza Cenci
Ministero di Grazia e Giustizia
Via d. Progresso
V. d. Tempio
Via Catalana
Portico d'Ottavia
Teatro di Marcello
Via dei Zoccolette
Piperno
V. B. Cenci
Sinagoga
Lungotevere dei Vallati
Lungotevere dei Cenci
Museo Ebraico di Roma
1
2
3
4
5

Stand beneath the **magnificent Pantheon dome** and be blessed with sunlight

You need to be in the Pantheon on a sunny day to appreciate its full celestial light. The oculus, a hole at the top of the dome, is its only source of illumination. When the sun shines, the intensely focused light pours in like a benediction, drawing your eyes heavenwards. Even on sunless days, the light feels ethereal.

The original building was raised in gratitude to the gods for Emperor Augustus's victory over Antony and Cleopatra. After it was damaged by fire, it was rebuilt in 126 AD by Emperor Hadrian, possibly to his own design. In 608, under the Emperor Phocas, the Pantheon was converted from a pagan temple to the church of St Mary of the Martyrs. This act most likely saved it from complete destruction, and it is now the best preserved ancient Roman building in the city.

This sacred resting place of painters (including Raphael) and rulers is a massive rotunda, with an imposing portico of 12m granite columns that once supported a huge pediment. The dome inspired Brunelleschi's Duomo in Florence and Michelangelo's St Peter's here in Rome.

Memorable days to visit are the summer solstice (20–21 June); Pentecost Sunday (seven weeks after Easter Sunday), when Mass ends with rose petals cascading through the dome; and Christmas Eve Mass when doves fly overhead.

For a romantic evening with the best view of the dome, take sunset *aperitivi* on the roof garden of the **Grand Hotel de la Minerve** (Piazza della Minerva 69; tel: 06-695 201; map G3).

Pantheon; Piazza della Rotonda; Mon–Sat 8.30am–7.30pm, Sun 9am–6pm; free; map F4

Treat yourself royally at Moriondo e Gariglio, **chocolatier to the House of Savoy**

Moriondo e Gariglio is Rome's chocolate maker to connoisseurs and kings. It started life in 1850 in Turin, serving the House of Savoy, and followed King Victor Emmanuel II here after unification 20 years later, making it the oldest chocolate shop in the city. Today, it is the official chocolatier to the Italian president.

The artisan confectioners adhere to family recipes passed down through the generations, and the shop is suitably ancient. The early Renaissance palazzo has exposed brick walls and arches highlighted in a Pompeiian red. The staff wear vintage lace aprons and caps, and wrap every item individually. Peruse the old-fashioned red and blue boxes in the antique display cabinets, and you will soon understand why Moriondo e Gariglio parcels are coveted.

Year-round favourites, such as chocolate-coated lemon and orange rinds, and candied cherries and fruits, are also accompanied by seasonal specialities. *Marrons glacés* decorate its autumn window, while candied violets (*violettes*) appear in late spring. Moriondo e Gariglio also makes the old-fashioned and usually hard-to-find *lacrime d'amore* (tears of love), tiny sugar tear-drops with a liquid centre. During the two weeks before Easter, the boutique is filled with *uova di Pasqua* (Easter eggs), as well as sugared lambs, fish, chicken and other animals.

If your sweet dreams remain unfulfilled, head to the other side of the Pantheon to **Gelateria della Palma** (Via della Maddalena 22; map F5), a neighbourhood ice creamery with a selection of cool delights.

Confetteria Moriondo e Gariglio; Via di Pie' di Marmo 21-2; tel: 06-699 0856; map G3

Discover the art of drinking **coffee *all'italiano*** at a quintessential Roman café

Ask an Italian to describe his or her perfect cup of coffee and you will get a passionate response. In Italy, coffee is an art form with many customs and traditions. Whether a creamy but quick cappuccino and *cornetto* (Italian croissant) at breakfast, a steamy shot of strong black espresso to recharge your batteries or a cooling *caffè shakerato* on a sweltering summer day, there is a coffee for every time and mood.

With an emphasis on taste, *il caffè* is serious business, and nowhere in Rome is the rivalry for perfection stronger than at Sant'Eustachio and Tazza d'Oro, neighbours in the Pantheon area.

For over 70 years, **Sant'Eustachio**, just behind the Pantheon, has been serving coffee to politicians, Roman residents and visitors. John F. Kennedy, Boris Yeltsin and many senators have been at the bar here, and though prices are high, the taste is worth the extra. The Ricci family slow roasts a blend on the premises using 100 percent fair-trade Arabica beans, such as green-tipped Bourbon from Saint Helena, Maragogype from Ecuador or Arabica and Old Bourbon from San Cristobal in the Galapagos.

COFFEE MENU

Espresso Also simply known as *caffè*, a short shot served in *demitasse* cups.
Caffè latte Espresso with less warm milk than a cappuccino, no foam, in a glass.
Cappuccino Equal parts espresso and foamed milk, served in a cappuccino cup.
Corretto Espresso that is 'corrected' with grappa, cognac or sambuca.
Doppio A double (or two shots) espresso.
Latte macchiato Steamed milk that is coloured with a shot of espresso.
Lungo or ***caffè americano*** Espresso with extra water.
Macchiato Espresso topped with a drop of steamed milk.
Ristretto A concentrated espresso made with less water.
Shakerato Espresso, sugar and ice, shaken until frothy, served in a flute.
Freddo (cold) Espresso, cappuccino and *corretto* can also be served cold.

The star of the line-up is their astoundingly thick *gran caffè*, a large and creamy espresso that is as beautiful to look at as it is good to drink.

To feel like a local, order your drink at the cashier opposite the bar, take your receipt to the *barista* and drink your coffee as Italians do – while standing.

Or else sit outside in the piazza where there is waiter service, which costs a little more and is more relaxed.

No matter what, hold fire before you add sugar to your coffee – the *baristi* follow the Neapolitan tradition of mixing a creamy sugar into the coffee.

On the opposite side of the Pantheon is **Tazza d'Oro**. The bar here is more of a people's café, with counter service only. Always crowded, and chaotic at times, the cashier queue moves fast, and what you get is worth the wait. Like Sant'Eustachio, Tazza d'Oro's reputation centres on the quality of its finely roasted coffee.

For €2.50, enjoy the hallowed tradition of a *granita di caffè con panna*. Made with a cupful of bittersweet frozen espresso, crushed to a slushy consistency and layered with fluffy clouds of whipped cream, the drink is perfect for Rome's hot summers or an after-dinner dessert.

Sant'Eustachio; Piazza Sant'Eustachio 81; www.santeustachioilcaffe.it; tel: 06-688 02048; daily 8.30am–1am; map F4
Tazza d'Oro; Via degli Orfani 84; www.tazzadorocoffeeshop.com; tel: 06-678 9792; daily 7.30am–1am ; map G4

Meander through the **backstreets of Piazza Navona** for **antiques, original designs and vintage finds**

The medieval side streets in the neighbourhood that lies behind Piazza Navona are full of intriguing shops selling antiques, bric-a-brac and memorabilia alongside cutting-edge designer clothing, artworks and jewellery. This is a place to become happily lost for an hour or two.

Starting at the southern end of Piazza Navona, at Piazza Pasquino, say hello to Pasquino, the first of the city's 'talking statues', on whom disgruntled citizens used to post criticism of the authorities *(see p. 60)*. Head west on Via del Governo Vecchio to find quaint shops for jewellery, personal and home accessories. Take a peek at the rock-and-roll jewellery of House of Fendi granddaughter **Delfina Delettrez** (67), and visit **Martino Midali** (105) for chic clothing from Milan. There's more to look at on Via del Governo Vecchio up to the beautiful Renaissance Piazza dell'Orologio, noted for its clock tower.

If you turn right on Via degli Orsini, then take a left then a right down Vicolo Domizio, you will have walked around the Palazzo Orsini Taverna, a medieval fort then Renaissance palace. The Via dei Coronari is the road in front, lined with antique shops. Browse Italian Depression-era wooden furniture at **Giuliano Giorgi** (235) or Biedermeier furniture at **Verdini Antichita** (Via G. Zanardelli 6). Stop at **Milena Tranca** (230) for retro toys. And while strolling, treat yourself to an ice cream from the best parlour in Rome, **Gelateria al Teatro** (Via di San Simone 70) with such tantalising flavours as Sicilian blood orange, sage and raspberry and *granita di limone* (crushed lemon ice).

Piazza Pasquino; map E3
Via del Governo Vecchio E3–D4
Via dei Coronari; map C5–D5

Find a **hidden Raphael** and enjoy breakfast in the cloisters of **Santa Maria della Pace**

The rounded portico of Santa Maria della Pace, designed by Pietro da Cortona in the 1660s, is bound to catch your eye as you meander through the streets behind Piazza Navona. But like many churches in Rome, it's not easy to visit. Theoretically, it is open twice a week for two hours, but this depends on the whim of the key holder.

The reward for your patience is Raphael's *Quattro Sibille* above the private chapel of Agostino Chigi, a patron of the Renaissance. One of Raphael's three commissions from the banker of Rome, this masterpiece was painted in 1514 with four robust and expressive sibyls, one of them pictured here above the entrance to the chapel.

Next door is the unexpected bonus of the **Chiostro del Bramante**, a two-storey, white marble cloister hiding not just an exhibition space and bookstore but one of the few decent breakfast spots in Rome. Contrary to Rome's traditional coffee and pastry fare, the Chiostro serves a delectable, protein-inspired brunch with designer omelettes, fried eggs, *friselle* (crunchy bread), baguettes and carpaccios. Here you can contemplate like a monk, on a narrow bench built into the walls of the cloister, which was designed by Donato Bramante in 1500, or at a comfortable modern table.

Santa Maria della Pace; Arco della Pace 5; 06-686 1156; Tue and Thur 10–11am; map D4
Chiostro del Bramante: tel: 06-6880 9035; Tue–Sat 10am–7.30pm, Sun 10am–4pm

Raise a glass of **fine Italian wine** in an **authentic *enoteca***

An *enoteca* (wine bar) is the best place to learn about Italian wine. These distinctive neighbourhood establishments serve a wide variety of wine *in mescita* (by the glass), often on a rotating basis, and sometimes organise evening tastings. To accompany the wine, most bars have menus with delicious *antipasti*.

Two wine bars in the southern half of the Centro Storico stand out for their decidedly Roman ethos: Il Goccetto (the Drop) on Via dei Banchi Vecchi and L'Angolo Divino (the Divine Corner), just off Campo de' Fiori.

Beautifully decorated with floor-to-ceiling wine bottles complemented by a dark wood-beam ceiling, **Il Goccetto** is known for its extensive French and Italian wine selection and fabulous cheeses. Ask the owner Sergio for a sample of his *tomino* cheese with black truffle wrapped in leaves. It is not to be missed.

For something quieter, **L'Angolo Divino** on a side alley behind Campo de' Fiori is a cosy spot for whispered conversations, The owner will help you choose from his extensive collection of high-quality wines, including Barbaresco, Amarone, Prosecco, and Tocai from Italy's north and Sangiovese, Merlot, Nero D'avola and Primitivo from further south.

For something sophisticated, try **Casa Bleve**, a two-storey glass-topped courtyard with a lavish wine selection including a depth of vintages.

Il Goccetto; Via dei Banchi Vecchi 14; Mon–Sat 7pm–midnight; map C3
L'Angolo Divino; Via dei Balestrari 12; Tue–Sun 10am–2.30pm, 5pm–2am; map E2
Casa Bleve; Via del Teatro Valle 49; tel: 06-686 5970; Tue–Sat 12.30–3pm, 7.30–10.30pm; map F3

Enjoy a long, leisurely **dinner the local way** in a picturesque piazza at **Maccheroni**

A night out to a Roman means two- to three-hour-long dinners of authentic cooking and excellent wines, beginning no earlier than 8.30pm. For a typical local experience, reserve a ground-floor table at Ristorante Maccheroni at 9pm – indoors in cold weather or outdoors in warm. Maccheroni is picture-perfect with a simple decor of wooden tables and white-paper tablecloths, and bottle-filled shelves along whitewashed walls.

Key to dining like a Roman is to know exactly what you want, even before looking at the menu. The hands-down favourite here is *rigatoni alla gricia* (bacon, Pecorino cheese and black pepper), or try Maccheroni's speciality, *trofie* – short, twisted pasta with black truffle sauce. The meat cuts are excellent, like the *tagliata con rughetta*, a juicy steak, thinly sliced and served on rocket. In autumn and early spring, Maccheroni serves Rome's favourite green vegetable, *puntarelle*, tender chicory stems, in a garlic, olive oil and anchovy dressing.

Piazza delle Coppelle is famous for its morning flower and fruit market, a picturesque scene from 8am to noon. In the early evening, the wine barrels in front of **Vinoteca Novecento** (47; 06-683 3078; map F5) are buzzing with guests of the *enoteca*. And in the later evening hours, after-dinner drinks are a must at **Le Coppelle** (52; map F5), a tiny bar on a prime piazza site.

Ristorante Maccheroni; Piazza delle Coppelle 44; tel: 06-6830 7895; www.ristorantemaccheroni.com; daily 1–3pm, 8pm–midnight; map F5

Discover **three Caravaggio masterpieces** in the superb rococo **church of San Luigi dei Francesi**

During his 11 years in Rome, Michelangelo Merisi (1571–1610), known as Caravaggio after his home town near Milan, rose from lowly apprentice to highly-paid painter and bad boy. Violent and argumentative, he fled Rome after killing a man in a brawl in 1606. What Caravaggio left behind were rich and realist paintings that set a benchmark in Western art.

Though his supporters were few, they were vocal and often wealthy, high-ranking Vatican clergy and noblemen among them. In 1599 the French Cardinal Matthieu Cointrel (Contarelli) commissioned Caravaggio to paint a triptych of the life of St Matthew the Evangelist for San Luigi dei Francesi, a Baroque jewel between Piazza Navona and the Pantheon. The Contarelli chapel has three luminous masterpieces: *The Calling of St Matthew*, where a bare-foot Christ points to a surprised Matthew; *The Inspiration of St Matthew* (pictured here), as an angel appears to the saint; and *The Martyrdom of St Matthew*, where Caravaggio himself lurks behind St Matthew's assassin.

San Luigi dei Francesi; 5 Piazza San Luigi dei Francesi, Via Santa Giovanna d'Arco; tel 06-688 271; daily 7.30am–12.30pm, 3.30–7pm, closed Thur pm; map F4

A COIN FOR A CARAVAGGIO

Rome has 23 Caravaggio paintings, which can be found in the following galleries and churches:

Casino Ludovisi, Galleria Borghese *(p.126)*, Galleria Doria Pamphilj *(p.54)*, Musei Capitolini, Palazzo Barberini *(p.133)*, Palazzo Corsini *(p.112)* and the churches of San Agostino, Santa Maria della Concezione dei Cappuccini and Santa Maria del Popolo *(p.50)*.

Most collections have an entry fee and some require advance reservations. Churches are free but coins are often needed for lighting. Note that churches usually close between noon and 3.30pm.

Watch the **sun set on the domes of Rome** from the terrazzo of the **St George Hotel**

The 72 sparkling domes that are spread across the Eternal City's skyline make it an ideal place to witness the setting of the sun. But it can be problematic when you have to decide which dome to gaze upon as you sip your first *aperitivo*. This is easily solved by making a visit to the St George Hotel, a neoclassical boutique establishment on the elegant Via Giulia, between Campo de' Fiori and the River Tiber. Go up to the terrace lounge for a generous 360-degree view of the city, a panorama of domes, obelisks, towers and fountains.

Look westwards for the dome of St Peter's Basilica *(p.74)*, the lighthouse on the Gianicolo hill and Rome's largest fountain, the Fontanone *(p.100)*.

For a front-row view of Baroque and Renaissance architectural ornamentation, head to the eastern terrace, which overlooks the *palazzi* on the Via Giulia, a 16th-century papal road. From this terrace, you can study cornices, mouldings and medallions, and peek into the attic apartments and patios of the *haute bourgeoisie*.

The **Rooftop Lounge** has a bubble-inspired *aperitivo* of Champagne, Franciacorta and Prosecco, along with wines, rosés, beer and cocktails. The light fare menu includes traditional Roman-style antipasti such as *pizzette* (small pizzas), savoury tarts and olives, as well as oysters and other delectable seafood.

Rooftop Lounge at the St George Hotel; Via Giulia 62; tel 06-686 611; www.stgeorgehotel.it; May–Sept daily 7–11.30pm; map B4

Enjoy a **pampering** fit for an emperor – or a simple shave – at **Wonderfool**

Roman emperors spent hours, if not days, being spoiled with beauty secrets found in the four corners of the empire. Two thousand years later, modern-day Caligulas are still taking time off from the chaotic city for a simple shave and haircut.

On Via dei Banchi Vecchi, a side street between Piazza Navona and the River Tiber, is Wonderfool. With sauna and gym, this gentleman's hairdresser's has more on offer than just the vintage art of the barber.

The setting is perfect, an afternoon in a suave, James Bond-esque study of leather, dark wood and chrome. Here men, and only men, can request whatever grooming regime they would like – from a low-maintenance traditional shave to more fanciful massages and treatments – while reading the newspaper or having a cappuccino. A favourite among the overstressed is the 'Bamboo Massage', an Asian ritual where oil is massaged across the contours of the face using different-sized bamboo rods.

Though Wonderfool is billed as 'gentlemen only', every Tuesday the spa opens its doors to women who can enjoy beauty treatments designed specifically for them.

Of course, every emperor needs his accessories, so have a look round Wonderfool's small store, which sells handmade beauty products, shaving kits and cashmere robes.

Wonderfool; Via dei Banchi Nuovi 39; tel: 06-6889 2315; www.wonderfool.it; daily; map C4

Primp like an empress in an ancient Roman bathhouse at **women-only hammam, AcquaMadre**

Although the 2nd-century satirist Juvenal wrote, 'Rare is the union of beauty and purity', it is possible to achieve both at AcquaMadre, a beautiful Turkish bath or hammam hidden in the medieval alleys of the Ghetto. AcquaMadre, 'mother water' in Italian, devotes its Mondays and Fridays to women only, while the rest of week both men and women can soak together. Reminiscent of an ancient Roman *thermae*, the Turkish bath is simple in its design, and has exposed ancient brick walls and arches to encourage an ancient bathhouse ambience.

Purification of the mind as well as the body is the underlying theme here. The multi-room spa was designed for pampering and relaxing, as well as socialising, a fundamental element in antiquity's bathhouses. Taking its names from ancient Rome, the main room, the *tepidarium*, is heated to 36°C and is an open space with mosaic tables, benches and fountains where attendants wait on you hand and foot, pouring warm and cool water in anticipation of your personalised treatments. Around the *tepidarium* are the *calidarium* (hot steam) showers, *frigidarium* (cold bath), tea and relax rooms.

The more fabulous treatments include a full-body green clay mask, invigorating Dead Sea salt scrubs, and rejuvenating Dead Sea mud treatments. First-time visitors are given a 'basic kit' of flip-flops and scrub glove. Bathing costumes are required if visiting on mixed gender days.

AcquaMadre; Via di Sant'Ambrogio 17; tel: 06-686 4272; www.acquamadre.it; women: Mon, Fri 11am–9pm; mixed: Tue 2–9pm, Thur, Sat–Sun 11am–9pm; children (up to 6 years): first Tue of the month; map G1

Sip **freshly squeezed orange juice** and read the morning papers in **tranquil Piazza Farnese**

Spremuta di arancia, freshly squeezed orange juice, is one of Italy's morning pleasures. Almost every bar and café offers *spremuta*, with a price significantly higher than a cappuccino. Choosing how, where and when to enjoy your *spremuta* is important. High on the list is a pavement seat at Caffè Farnese, a lovely, gilded corner coffee shop in picturesque Piazza Farnese, next to the Campo de' Fiori.

In the early morning, when Campo de' Fiori vendors have finished primping their stands, **Caffè Farnese** opens its doors to its clientele of market-goers, neighbourhood socialites, shop owners, policemen and tourists. The indoor bar is always crowded, so take a seat outside and under an umbrella, especially in spring or summer. There is a well-stocked news kiosk beside the café's outside tables, with dailies, weeklies and monthlies in a number of languages. If you can't find your desired reading matter, walk over to Campo de' Fiori to the 'other' kiosk, which also has an in-depth selection of international publications.

Technically, a true *spremuta di arancia* is made on the spot, using standard oranges or blood oranges, which are in season from December to May: the full-blood *sanguinella*, the more bitter *Moro* and the prized *Tarocco* from Sicily.

Though delicious alone, non-purists often add a spoonful of sugar to cut the acidity. Be careful not to confuse it with the *succo di frutta*, a small bottle of processed fruit juice that will leave you unsatisfied when wanting freshly squeezed juice.

Caffè Farnese; Piazza Farnese, Via dei Baullari 106; tel: 06-688 02 125; daily 7am–midnight; map D2

Look heavenwards at the **lapis lazuli ceiling** of **Rome's only Gothic church**

To the left and behind the Pantheon is the seemingly non-descript Basilica of **Santa Maria Sopra Minerva**. What will first grab your attention is Minerva's Pulcino, the playful elephant and Egyptian obelisk outside the church designed by Gianlorenzo Bernini. But don't let the church's plain facade fool you; walk inside to find a rich interior under the city's only Gothic nave.

Built over a temple to the Roman goddess Minerva, Santa Maria Sopra Minerva has ogival (pointed) arches and ceiling vaulting. Painted lapis-blue with gold stars and giving the impression of a heavenly evening, the church is a wonderful sanctuary on a rainy day.

There is a variety of Renaissance and Baroque treasures and tombs, including that of fresco master Fra Angelico (1455). On the high altar is the sarcophagus (and headless remains) of Saint Catherine of Siena, patron saint of Italy. Immediately to the left of the main altar is a Michelangelo sculpture of Christ the Redeemer (1521), whose nudity shocked the church at the time. Carved as a nude figure in Florence, it was then sent to Rome where it was ineptly finished by pupils. It is probably the only opportunity to stand within arm's reach of the sculptor's work.

This was the main church of the Dominicans, principal prosecutors of the Inquisition. In the right aisle's penultimate chapel is the glorious *Annunciation* fresco by Antoniazzo Romano (1485). Beside the poor girls kneeling before the Madonna is the Inquisition's Cardinal Juan de Torquemada in uncharacteristically humble pose.

Santa Maria Sopra Minerva; Piazza della Minerva 42; tel: 06-679 3926; Mon–Sat 7am–7pm, Sun 8am–noon, 2–7pm; map G3

Sample **mouth-watering fried artichokes** and other Romano-Jewish delicacies in the **Ghetto**

Il Ghetto, a small quarter between the Via Arenula and the Teatro di Marcello, is home to one of Europe's oldest communities of Jewish families. This is a great place to find that unique hybrid, Roman-Jewish cuisine. Drawing upon the culturally diverse heritages at the foundation of Italikim (Italian area), Sephardic (Spanish) and Libyan culinary traditions, *cucina romana ebraica* developed its own identity, clinging to the traditions of the past and fusing them with ingredients available in Rome. The result is tempting dishes such as *carciofi alla giudia* (fried artichokes), *baccalà fritto alla giudia* (fried salt cod), and other unique kosher delicacies.

Favourite Ghetto eateries include the traditional **Da Giggetto** (Via del Portico d'Ottavio; tel: 06-686 1105; closed Mon; map G1). Make sure to sit in the back courtyard by the medieval walls. The more formal **Piperno** (Via Monte Cenci 9; tel: 06-6880 6629; closed Mon, and Sun pm; map F1) requires reservations and stylish dress. Finally, the very casual **Sora Margherita**, hidden behind a tiny door at Piazza delle Cinque Scole (30; tel: 06-687-4216; lunch only; map F1), serves simple and hearty fare. Reservations and a completed membership form are required.

If you don't have time for a meal, pop into **Pasticceria Zi Boccione** (Via Portico d'Ottavia 1; closed Sat; map F1), a closet-sized kosher pastry shop in the heart of the Ghetto, and queue with patrons of all religions. The sisters of Zi Boccione have been rolling out cinnamon almond *biscotti* and mouth-watering *pizza ebraica* (Jewish pizza – thick bricks of sweet dough stuffed with candied fruit, almonds, pine nuts and raisins) for as long as anyone can remember.

Enjoy an **elegant aperitif** away from the chaotic Campo de' Fiori at **Camponeschi**

The secret to a successful evening in the Campo de' Fiori area is to bypass the clamorous square and head for adjacent Piazza Farnese for a sunset spritzer or full-bodied Barolo at Camponeschi wine bar. Attached to Rome's historic Ristorante Camponeschi is this modern *enoteca,* which stocks French and Italian labels and serves contemporary snacks.

A NIGHT ON THE CAMPO

Campo de' Fiori is a magnet for the college-aged study abroad crowd. Most Romans tend to avoid the evening Campo, but expats and students favour the **Drunken Ship** (21–22) and 'sister bar' **Sloppy Sam's** (10) for nachos, martinis, beer and all-around disorder, while the more posh inebriated prefer rustic **Baccanale** (32), modish 'mozzarella bar' **Obika** (corner Via dei Baullari) or quaint **Il Nolano** (11), whether for *aperitivi* or after-dinner drinking.

Whether they've come for the wines, antipasti or the juicy green olives, guests crowd the enoteca at 7pm, spilling out of the bar, past the umbrellas into the piazza.

To the right of the wine bar is the regal Palazzo Farnese, now the French Embassy, a high-Renaissance building to which Michelangelo added the upper floors. Directly opposite is Santa Brigida (at 96), with a picturesque bell tower.

Camponeschi's restaurant offers great fish dishes such as the lobster, black truffle and raspberry vinegar appetiser. Or head across the piazza to **Ar Galletto** (tel: 06-686 1714), a traditional Roman trattoria with a fabulous carbonara and chicken dishes.

Camponeschi; Piazza Farnese 50–51; tel: 06-687 4927; Mon–Sat 7–10.30pm; map D2

Take a **romantic evening stroll** among the illuminated fountains of **Piazza Navona**

The most favourite pastime in Rome is the evening *passeggiata*, a pre- or post-dinner stroll around any piazza or park. And the prize for the most picturesque and romantic place for a sunset *passeggiata* is Piazza Navona. Built on a 1st-century stadium, it glows a warm orange and is serenaded by local musicians.

In the centre are three fountains: Fontana di Nettuno (Fountain of Neptune), Fontana dei Quattro Fiumi (Fountain of the Four Rivers) and Fontana del Moro (Fountain of the Moor), masterpieces of nymphs, gods and mermen that mix beauty with humour.

The Fontana dei Quattro Fiumi *(pictured)* by Gianlorenzo Bernini, from around 1645, is worth a full tour. It depicts four rivers – the Danube, Ganges, Nile and Plate – as allegorical figures who also represent four continents: Europe, Asia, Africa and America. The Nile is blindfolded because the source of the river was then still a mystery. Rising above the statues is an obelisk taken from the Circus of Maxentius. It is topped by the figure of a dove with an olive branch to show that this once pagan monument has been converted into a Christian one.

Tucked behind Piazza Navona is **Santa Lucia** (Largo Febo 12; tel: 06-6880 2427; map E4), a quiet restaurant with cuisine from the Amalfi Coast. The menu has a selection of fish-inspired dishes, and is known for its wonderful *ovoli* (Julius Caesar's favourite mushrooms) and parmesan shard salad. For rainy evenings, head to **Orso 80** (Via dell' Orso; tel 06-686 4904; map E5) just north of Piazza Navona, which also specialises in fish dishes.

Piazza Navona; map E4

Discover the **tucked-away Napoleonic Museum** to see the **treasures of the Bonapartes**

In a narrow Baroque palazzo by the River Tiber is the Palazzo Primoli, once home to Napoleon Bonaparte's grandnephew and now the Napoleonic Museum. It contains a personal collection of relics bequeathed to the city by Count Giuseppe Primoli, son of Princess Carlotta Bonaparte, in 1927. Primoli's wish was to show the relationship between the Bonapartes and Rome.

In 1808 the French army occupied Rome and plundered its treasures, but after Napoleon's defeat at Waterloo seven years later almost all of the House of Bonaparte settled in the Eternal City, including Napoleon's mother, brothers and sister Pauline. Thus, years later, grandnephew Giuseppe inherited a collection of imperial knick-knacks which are testament to French splendour in Rome.

The Palazzo Primoli remains in late 19th-century lavish decor, a perfect complement to its vast array of artefacts, including imperial busts, canvases, miniatures, clothing and silver that herald the First and Second French Empires. The rounded plaster cast is the cast of the breast of Pauline.

Museo Napoleonico; Piazza di Ponte Umberto I 1; tel: 06-687 4240; www.museonapoleonico.com; Tue–Sun 9am–7pm; charge; map E5

THE EMPEROR'S RISQUÉ SISTER
This painting of Pauline Bonaparte, hanging in the Museo Napoleonico, is by François Joseph Kinson, and it makes her look demure. She was anything but. In August 1803 Napoleon's sister secretly wed Camillo Borghese in an effort to build ties towards French-occupied Italy - and enjoy the Borghese wealth. Her husband commissioned Antonio Canova to sculpt her, for which she posed nude. The resulting life-size *Venus Victrix* was far too risqué for Roman society and it was kept out of sight. Today it resides in Galleria Borghese *(see p. 126)*.

Tridente and Trevi

Tridente and Trevi

E
F
G
H
5
4
3
2
1
Frette
Via San Sebastiano
Il Palazzetto
Piazza di Spagna
SPAGNA
SS. Trinità dei Monti
Piazza Trinità dei Monti
Sermoneta
Hassler
René Caovilla
Piazza Mignanelli
Palazzo Spagna
Alexander
Via Frattina
Propaganda Fide
Via Gregoriana
Via Sistina
Via F. Crispi
C. le Case
Due Macelli
Casa Howard
S. Andrea d. Fratte
Via d. Mercede
Via Nazareno
Largo del Tritone
Via del Tritone
Via Zucchelli
V. Cappuccini
Casa Howard
Piazza Barberini
BARBERINI/ FONT. TREVI
Via Veneto
Via Liguria
V. degli Artisti
Santa Marina d. Concezione
Via Molise
Via Versilia
Via Leonida Bissolati
Via San Basilio
Via Santa Nicola de Tolention
Salita di Santa Nicola da Tolentio
Via Barberini
Palazzo Barberini (Galleria Natzionale d'Arte Antica)
Via XX Settembre
Via d. Avignonesi
Daphne Inn
Kami Spa
Via Rasella
Via delle Quattro Fontane
V. Serviti
V. del Traforo
Colline Emiliane
V. dei Maroniti
Via d. Panetteria
Via Scuderie
S. Claudio
Palazzo Poli
S. Maria in Via
Fontana di Trevi (Trevi Fountain)
Via d. Lavatore
GIARDINO DEL QUIRINALE
Museo Naz. d. Paste Alimentari
Palazzo del Quirinale
Via d. Muratte
V. d. Vergini
Via della Dataria
Via Lucchesi
Via dell'Umiltà
Via dell' Archetto
Piazza del Quirinale
S. Marcello
Antica Birreria Peroni
Piazza Pilotta
Scuderie del Quirinale
Via XXIV Maggio
Palazzo Odescalchi
SS. Apostoli
VILLA COLONNA
Piazza dei SS. Apostoli
Palazzo Colonna
S. Silvestro

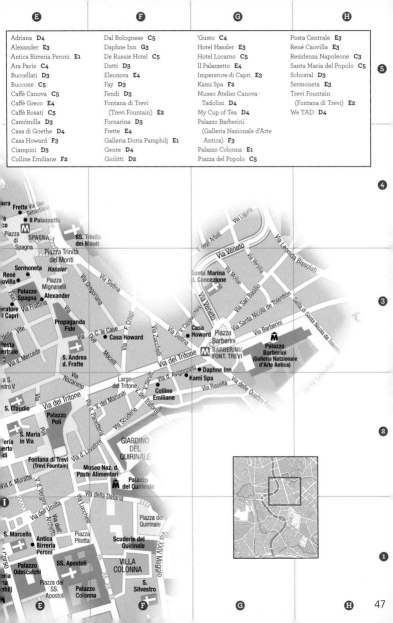

Vhile breakfast in Rome can be
ı brief exercise in personal space,
vying for a cappuccino and pastry
ıt the local bar, the Roman brunch
s an altogether more leisurely
esson in style. The chic, family-
ɔwned Caffè Ciampini holds court
n a quiet square where any day of
he week politicians and patricians,
ırtists, activists and office workers
enjoy light fare.

Although it is just off the Via
lel Corso, Rome's busiest street,
he manicured Piazza San Lorenzo
n Lucina is a calm backwater.
Here nattily dressed parents chat
vhile well-pressed children run
ınboisterously, the fur-clad toy-dog
set sip Prosecco, and hand-tailored
gentlemen exchange political
gossip and advice on grooming.
You are more likely to overhear
nultilingual
discussions
ıbout politics,
iterature and
education
than directions to the nearest
monument.

Caffè Ciampini has a satisfying brunch/light lunch menu of salads, sandwiches and pasta dishes. Of particular excellence is the club sandwich, a refined double-layer white-bread *tramezzino* with eggs and cornichons. In summer, enjoy the home-made iced tea and *gelati*, including the superb chocolate variety. From November to February, the hot chocolate with fresh whipped cream is ideal to ward off the cold. If it is raining or too chilly, head upstairs to Caffè Ciampini's rustic tea salon.

The best time for people-watching? Try lunch (around 1pm) or *aperitivi* hours (from 6pm).

Ciampini; Piazza San Lorenzo in Lucina 29; tel: 06-687 6606; www.ciampini.net; Mon–Sat 7.30am–7.30pm; map D3

Examine **Caesar Augustus' 1st-century BC altar** in its 21st-century AD home at the **Ara Pacis**

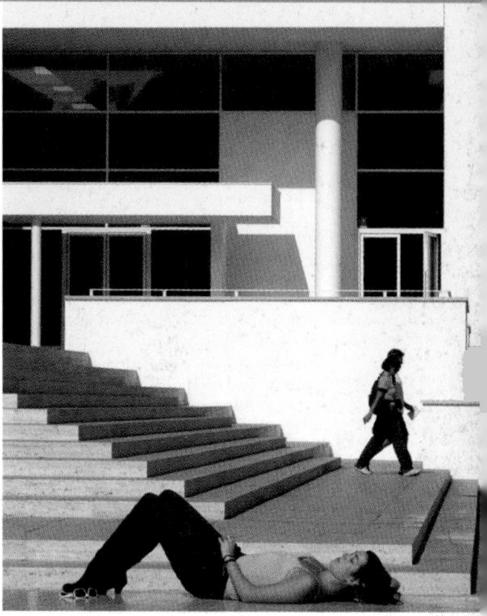

One of Rome's most important monuments is the Ara Pacis, a 1st-century-BC 'Altar of Peace', housed in Richard Meier's purpose-built glass-and-travertine museum. The altar, which was used for sacrifices, comemmorates Caesar Augustus, Rome's first and most powerful emperor, who ruled from 27 BC to 14 AD, extending *Pax Romana* to its furthest corners of Europe and the Mediterranean.

Surrounding the altar is a richly decorated white marble wall with friezes depicting 100 figures, including the imperial family in procession. Coloured lights are occasionally projected onto the altar to show how it would have appeared in antiquity.

Res Gestae Divi Augusti (The Deeds of the Divine Augustus) is inscribed on the outside of the museum. This first-person account of the life of the emperor, the adopted son of Julius Caesar, explains the origins of the dynasty; elsewhere, the family tree is laid out with imperial portrait casts.

Meier's minimal box was hugely controversial when it opened in 2006. By contrast, across the Via di Ripetta are the decaying ruins of the huge mausoleum that Augustus built for himself, but this is not open to the public.

For those craving a good Roman pizza, walk to the other side of the Mausoleum of Augustus to find **'Gusto** (Piazza Augusto Imperatore 9; tel: 06-6322 6273; map C3) in the Fascist-era Piazza Augusto Imperatore. In the same building, but behind it on Via della Frezza, is Gusto's cheese bar, while at Piazza Augusto Imperatore 28 is Gusto's fish-inspired trattoria. All very good.

Ara Pacis, Lungotevere in Augusta at via Tomacelli; tel: 06-8205 9127; www.arapacis.it; Tue–Sun 9am–7pm; charge; map C4

Watch the action in the magnificent **Piazza del Popolo** from the Pincio Terrace

Piazza del Popolo, the 'People's Square', is one of Rome's largest open areas and the traditional forecourt to the city, which means this is the best place to spy a slice of daily life. And there is no better viewing point than the panoramic **Pincio Terrace**, at the top of the steps that lead up from **Santa Maria del Popolo**. The finest artworks to behold in this treasure-filled church are two luminous paintings by Caravaggio – *The Conversion of St Paul* and *The Crucifixion of St Peter* – which attest to the painter's genius.

The church flanks Porto del Popolo (also known as Porta Flaminia), the entrance gate incorporated into the 3rd-century AD Aurelian walls.

The square marks the top of the Tridente (the Trident), an area formed by the three major roads into the city: Via di Ripetta, Via del Corso and Via del Babuino. These converge on the south side of the square, at the junction of the twin churches of Santa Maria in Montesanto and Santa Maria dei Miracoli, dating from the 1660s.

Piazza del Popolo was given its present grandeur by the architect Giuseppe Valadier in 1822, his sweeping double semicircles echoing Bernini's colonnades that embrace St Peter's Square.

The extensive piazza can contain thousands of people, making it a natural venue for concerts and exhibitions, performances and flashmobs, as well as international celebrations and ceremonies like World Cups and papal coronations when crowds gather in front of large screens. Each month seems to bring an event or exhibition, and from April to September there is a free concert almost every weekend.

'Meet me at the obelisk' means a rendezvous at the piazza's central fountain, and this is where you will find Roman children, tired tourists and the odd busker. Four lions guard a 24m-high obelisk, brought to Rome by Augustus

Caesar in 10 BC after his conquest of Egypt and originally placed in the Circus Maximus.

On either side of the southern curve are the piazza's two famous feuding cafés – left-wing **Rosati** (tel: 06-322 5859) and right-wing **Canova** (tel: 06-361 3231), whose regulars from the film world once included directors Federico Fellini (Rosati) and Pier Pasolini (Canova). Today, choice in where you enjoy your afternoon coffee or evening *aperitivo* is based less on ideology and more on how much sun you'd like to soak in.

Locals love to lunch or dine at **Buccone** on Via di Ripetta (19; tel 06-361 2154; closed Sun; map C5), a turn-of-the-century wine, spirits and confectionery shop with a tiny dining area.

Piazza del Popolo; map C5

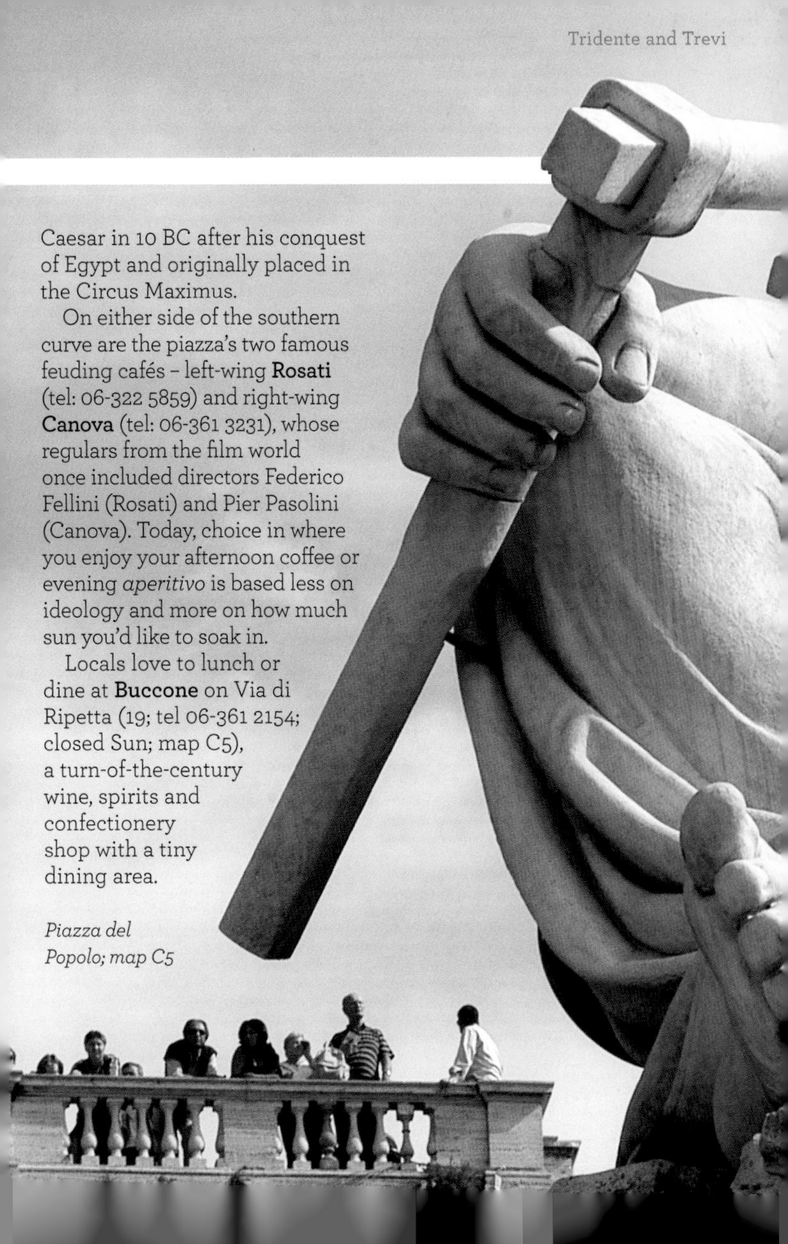

Savour a **private view of the Spanish Steps** at the Palazzetto's wine bar

The sweeping Spanish Steps combine with the twin towers of Trinità dei Monti above and the harmonious square below to form one of the most distinctive of Roman scenes. Piazza di Spagna gets its name from the Spanish Embassy to the Holy See, which has been here since the 17th century.

The cascading steps are perennially crowded with visitors, who share the steps with pots of azaleas in spring. The best place to make Piazza di Spagna all yours is the fifth-floor terrace of **Il Palazzetto**, the Hotel Hassler-owned boutique hotel, restaurant and wine bar. The small terrace, entered via a catwalk at the top of the Spanish Steps, is one of the highest in the neighbourhood, and overlooks the whole Piazza di Spagna.

The bar seats only 50 people and is simply decorated, since the multicoloured sunset backdrop of Renaissance palaces and dome of St Peter's Basilica are the only necessary decorations when sipping a delicious cocktail.

The *stuzzichini* (snacks) menu is light, but there is an evening buffet in the warmer months. On autumn and winter days, the terrace is open for daytime cocktails: keep one eye upwards to check it's open.

The **International Wine Academy of Roma** (tel: 06-699 0878; www.wineacademyroma.com) is on the ground floor of the Palazzetto and offers intimate, half-day courses on Italian wines. See their calendar for speciality programmes and masterclasses.

Il Palazzetto; Vicolo del Bottino 8; tel: 06-6993 41000; www.ilpalazzettoroma.com; Tue–Sun 6pm–midnight; check for autumn and winter daytime hours; map E4

Join the Grand Tour and follow in the footsteps of **great literary visitors** to Rome

The term 'Grand Tour' was the invention of Richard Lassels, an English Catholic priest. In 1670 he published *Voyage through Italy* in which he declared that 'young lords' should travel to France and Italy to get to know classical culture and the state of the world.

But it wasn't until the arrival of English Romantic poets Keats, Shelley *(pictured)* and Byron in the early 19th century that Rome was put firmly on the literary map. John Keats spent the last months of his 26th year in an apartment on Piazza di Spagna and is buried in the Protestant Cemetery *(p.160)*, where Percy Bysshe Shelley's ashes were placed after drowning at sea.

Keats's apartment, now the **Keats-Shelley Memorial House**, subsequently became a place of pilgrimage, attracting such literary luminaries as William Wordsworth and Oscar Wilde.

Across the piazza and just down the Via dei Condotti is the **Caffè Greco**, dating from 1760, which Wolfgang Goethe made *the* café for the Grand Tour intellectual. Every literary and cultural figure who ever visited the city, from Hans Christian Andersen to Henry James to Charles Baudelaire, came here. Try the *granita di caffè con panna*, crushed frozen espresso with cream.

At the end of Via dei Condotti, is the **Casa di Goethe** where Goethe stayed during visits in the late 18th century. You can peruse his journals and a room dedicated to all his works inspired by or written in Rome.

Keats-Shelley House; Piazza di Spagna 26; tel: 06-678 4235; www.keats-shelley-house.org; Mon–Fri 10am–1pm, 2–6pm, Sat 11am–2pm; charge; map E3
Caffè Greco; Via dei Condotti 86; tel: 06-679 1700; Mon–Sat 9am–7.30pm; map E4
Casa di Goethe; Via del Corso 18; tel: 06-3265 0412; Tue–Sun 10am–6pm; map C5

Take a **tour of a privately owned palazzo** and gaze at the grandeur of **Galleria Colonna's Great Hall**

Nowhere in the city feels as decadent as standing under the ceiling frescoes in the Great Hall of the Galleria Colonna, in Palazzo Colonna. Richly coloured and detailed images of the victory of the 1571 Battle of Lepanto, in which *pater familias* Marcantonio Colonna II commanded the papal fleet, span the majestic ceiling vault that stretches for 76m by 12m. Emulating the grandeur of Versailles, the 10m-high gallery is hung floor to ceiling with nearly 200 paintings, and decorated with painted mirrors, gilded moulding and Venetian chandeliers.

Look down as well as up: embedded into the steps of the Great Hall is a cannonball shot from the Gianicolo during the 1849 French siege of Rome.

The six-room gallery is the gem of Rome's private art collections, with such masterpieces as Bronzino's sensuous *Venus and Cupid*, and Annibale Caracci's much reproduced *Bean-Eater*.

The illustrious Colonna family, who have lived in the palace compound for 23 generations, are still in residence, and the gallery is open for visits only on Saturday mornings.

Galleria Colonna; Via della Pilotta 17; tel: 06-678 4350; www.galleriacolonna.it; Sat 9am–1pm; charge; map E1

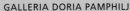

GALLERIA DORIA PAMPHILJ

The Galleria Doria Pamphilj (Via del Corso; www.doriapamphilj.it; tel: 06-679 7323; daily 10am–5pm; charge; map E1) has an extensive array of furniture and statuary, and the best painting collection of all Rome's *palazzi*. Head for the Gallery of the Mirrors to see Diego Velazquez's mid-17th-century portrait of the Pamphilj pope. To complete a Caravaggio quest *(p.34)*, visit the next two rooms, where the *Penitent Magdalene, Rest on the Flight into Egyp*t and *St John the Baptist* hang.

Galleria Doria Pamphilj occasionally hosts classical concerts.

Forget fancy cocktails and quench your thirst with a **beer** at the **Antica Birreria Peroni**

Antica Birreria Peroni is the obvious pit stop for those in need of a lager or a beer. 'As precious as milk' reads the motto on the wall of the *birreria* that serves Peroni's Gran Riserva, Nastro Azzurro and Crystal Red as well as Fuller's London Pride from copper vats and on tap.

More than a century old, this is the original Peroni beer house. Though great-grandfather to and inspiration for the boutique Emporio Peroni, the Birreria's style is strictly turn-of-the-20th century with original Art Nouveau frescoes, brass ornaments and old-fashioned wooden tables and booths.

The recommended drinks are Peroni Nastro Azzurro or the double malt Peroni Gran Riserva, which are as smooth and sweet as lemonade on a hot day. The *birreria* is regarded as Rome's best place for hot dogs – there are eight different kinds with 14 variations. The Kilometre, a house speciality, is a rite of passage for the first-time guest or recently graduated student. Waiters sing and the crowd chants as you are served these whopping sausages.

For those in search of more inspiring food, the menu also has a selection of typical Roman dishes, such as fried antipasti, *scamorze* (smoked cheese), simple pasta dishes like *spaghetti alla carbonara*, and grilled meats, along with beerhouse favourites like goulash, sauerkraut, and hamburgers and chips.

For a broader range of beers, Trastevere's **Bir & Fud** and **Ma Che Siete Venuti A Fa'** *(p.107)* have scores of artisanal brews from across Europe.

Antica Birreria Peroni; Via di San Marcello 19; tel: 06-679 5310; www.anticabirreriaperoni.net; Mon–Sat noon–midnight; map E1

Blow the budget on a **hand-stitched Fendi handbag** at the shopping Mecca of the **Via dei Condotti**

The crossroads of Via dei Condotti and Via del Corso marks the glittering intersection between designer de luxe shops and trendy boutiques. This is the place to fire up your shopping engines, starting at the **Fendi** flagship store (Largo Goldoni; map D3). Take a peek inside Palazzo Fendi whether you are interested in haute couture or high-end interior design. The architect, Peter Marino, reconfigured the interior of the four-storey palazzo with a mix of classical and modern.

Just around the corner and across the street is **Fay** (Via Fontanella di Borghese 56; map D3), Italy's favourite shop for winter and spring jackets.

From here, head east on the Via dei Condotti. This is Rome's sunset strip, where fashion's usual suspects reign – Ferragamo, Bulgari, Louis Vuitton, Max Mara, Prada, Hermes, Gucci and Yves Saint Laurent – but it's the side streets where fashionistas find unique treasures. For baubles, bangles and bling, **Buccellati** (Via dei Condotti 31A; D3) has the real deal, or for fanciful *faux* try **Imperatore di Capri** (Via Mario dei Fiori 6a; E3). Delectable handmade handbags are found at **Dotti** (Via Belsiana 6; D3), while eye-popping shoes decorate the window of **Renè Caovilla** (Via Borgognona 9; E3).

Eventually all roads in this neighbourhood flow into Piazza di Spagna *(p.52)*. Shops on the square include the south-side **Sermoneta** (61; map E3) for quality gloves, **Alexander** (51; map E3) for designer jeans and other clothing, and **Frette** (Via San Sebastianello 5; E4) at the northern end for luxurious linens. In between are catwalk favourites Missoni, Gianfranco Ferre, Dolce & Gabbana and Sergio Rossi.

> **VIA DEL CORSO**
> The 1.5km-long strip between Piazza del Popolo and Piazza Venezia is the Via del Corso, the the 3rd-century BC Via Lata that led north to Rimini. The Corso is the shopping street for after-school and university crowds. Highlights include Milan's Hello Kitty emporium **Camomilla** (11), the flirtatious frock shop **Fornarina** (109) and **Schostal** (158), the 140-year-old cotton and cashmere boutique (map D3 for all).

The best shopping advice for the die-hard spender or avid window-shopper is to head north on Via del Babuino towards Piazza del Popolo. Named after the Babuino (Baboon), one of the 16th-century 'talking statues' *(p.60)*, this is the super-posh shopping road where Valentino, Belstaff, Chanel and MiuMiu are found happily rubbing shoulders with concept stores **Eleonora** (97; map E4) for fabulous women's clothing and shoes; **Gente** (81; map D4) for men and women's designer clothes, by appointment; **My Cup of Tea** (65; D4) for one-of-a-kind and boutique clothing, accessories and interior decorations; **Adriana** (59; map D4), a shoe heaven; and **We TAD** (155; map D4), for clothing, shoes and homewares.

Spoil yourself with a **rejuvenating massage** at **Kami Spa**

Relaxation has become a buzz word in Rome, inspiring a crop of spas catering to all kinds of beauty whims. Kami Spa is one of the newest and most luxurious. Labelling itself as a 'Gateway to Asia', it has a list of treatments representing the cultures and healing techniques of Japan, China, Indonesia and India.

The spa 'menu' is a gourmet listing of scrubs, masks, massages and facials. Scrub treatments are delectable: Coffee Bean, Lemon Grass, Cinnamon Clove and refreshingly *piccante* Wasabi Cream Polish – a wasabi, almond, jojoba oils and milk cleansing. Kami's Mom Care provides massages, scrubs and facials for expecting and new mothers. These include the exotic Black Sesame Benefits sesame-seed scrub with massage and the Moisture Dew facial. Alternatively, the Green Tea Body Cocoon, a 50-minute antioxidant body mask, will wash away a long day of touring Rome.

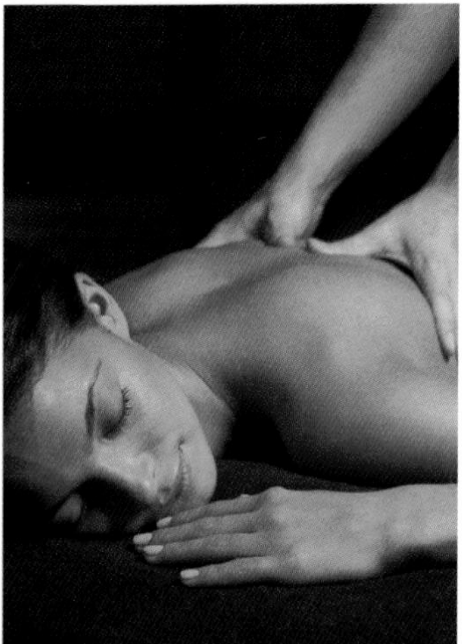

Massages include traditional, shiatsu, Thai and hot stones. Kami has also created out-of-body journeys – three-and-a-half hours of massages, scrubs and facials. Kami's signature Ayurlomi massage is a mix of meditative massages where your *dosha* (psychological energy) is identified and treated with essential oils.

All 60 rooms in this Baroque palazzo below Piazza Barberini are dedicated to treatments. The ground floor is a Zen sanctuary, with an *onsen*, a mineral water pool, beneath a four-storey atrium.

The Wellness Zone of the **Hotel de Russie** *(p.172)* is also recommended.

Kami Spa; Via degli Avignonesi 12; tel: 06-4201 0039; www.kamispa.com; Sun–Thur 10am–10pm, Fri, Sat 10am–midnight; map F2

Take advantage of a **quiet view of the Trevi Fountain** at night or at sunrise

As an essential sight of the Eternal City, the Trevi Fountain always has a deluge of visitors around its steps, taking photos and throwing pennies in its grandiose basin. Though tossing a coin ensures a return to Rome, fighting the masses is far from enchanting and may result in a quick exit out of the neighbourhood.

Nearly 30m high and 20m long, the Trevi Fountain takes up the entire southern wall of Palazzo Poli and is the result of nearly a century of ideas from artists including Pietro da Cortona and Gianlorenzo Bernini, with a final design by Nicola Salvi in 1762. Sculpted from travertine, the fountain celebrates the Acqua Virgo, the 1st-century aqueduct that brought water to the city from a spring 26km away. Its story can be seen in the two panels on the palazzo wall, while the young Virgo on a relief points to the source of the water.

At the centre of the fountain Neptune, god of water and the sea, stands on a large shell above two horses, one wild, the other calm, handled by Tritons, as water cascades bountifully around them.

In the late evening, when there are few people around, the dark sky reflects in the fountain's basin, the cobblestones glisten and the white marble glows from the streetlights, setting the stage for a perfect romantic moment. Catching the Trevi Fountain at sunrise is magnificent, too. And bear in mind that on Mondays the fountain is drained for coin collection, when the piazza becomes unexpectedly quiet.

Fontana di Trevi; map E2

Study the **casts of Canova with a coffee** in the Tadolini artists' studio caffè

The Museo Atelier Canova Tadolini is the only artists' studio in Rome where you can dip a croissant in a cappuccino while standing next to casts of monumental sculpture. The atelier was the workshop of Antonio Canova (1757–1822), the neoclassical sculptor from Venice who was famous for his nudes, especially the incomparable *Three Graces*. He bequeathed his moulds to his protégé Adamo Tadolini who then handed them on, together with his own, to his sons, who were also sculptors.

The copies are jumbled together in the enticing labyrinth of the museum-cum-café. On the ground floor is a beautifully kept turn-of-the-20th-century brass bar, while the upstairs wooden alcove has restaurant seating, acoustically satisfying on a rainy day. Casts not to be missed include Canova's Pauline Bonaparte as *Venus Victrix* (the original is at the Galleria Borghese, *p.126*) and the equestrian *Simon Bolivar* (in Caracas).

Museo Atelier Canova Tadolini; Via del Babuino 150a; tel: 06-3211 0702; www.museoateliercanovatadolini.it; Mon–Sat 8am–8.30pm; map D4

TALKING STATUES

Greeting passers-by on the Via del Babuino is the Babuino, one of Rome's five 'talking statues'. Babuino and his comrades Pasquino (Piazza di Pasquino), Marforio (Musei Capitolini), Abate Luigi (near Campo dei Fiori) and Madama Lucrezia (Piazza San Marco near Piazza Venezia) were 1st-century statuary uncovered in the early Renaissance. After their installation in the 16th century, anonymous political criticism and irreverent satire began to appear around each statue – poetry and witticisms voicing citizens' concerns and disagreements. The Pasquino *(p.30)* remains alone as Rome's critic, as the rest have been cleaned up and are off-limits.

See and be seen, and enjoy delightful **Emiliana-Romagnola cuisine**, at Dal Bolognese

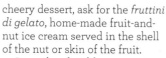

The clientele at **Dal Bolognese**, the celebrity restaurant on the southwest curve of Piazza del Popolo, dresses to impress and jackets are required for men. Reservations are hard to obtain, not just because the rich and famous pepper its patio, but because its Emiliana-Romagnola cuisine and service are renowned.

The key to true enjoyment here is to order the assortment of pastas *(misto di pasta)*, four mini-portions of pastas that include their famous *tortelloni con ricotta e spinaci* (large pasta stuffed with spinach and ricotta). The *astice alla catalana* (grilled lobster) is a *secondo* delicacy that should not be overlooked. For a light and cheery dessert, ask for the *fruttini di gelato*, home-made fruit-and-nut ice cream served in the shell of the nut or skin of the fruit.

At weekends tables are easier to acquire than in the evenings, otherwise you might have to sacrifice people-watching for the upstairs dining rooms.

Emilia-Romagna produces the ultimate comfort food. The region's rich, savoury dishes are the envy of the peninsula and Rome has two of the very best *cucina Emiliana Romagnola* restaurants in Dal Bolognese and the more casual, intimate and less expensive **Colline Emiliane**. For antipasto here try *culatello di Zibello*, a famous prosciutto from a town near Parma; for a *primo*, try *tortelli di zucca* (pumpkin stuffed pasta); and for *secondo*, *giambonnetto*, roast veal cooked in milk with potato purée. Finish with home-made zabaglione, whipped egg yolks with sugar and liqueur.

Dal Bolognese; Piazza del Popolo 1; tel: 06-361 1426; Tue–Sun 1–3pm, 8.15pm–midnight; map C5
Colline Emiliane; Via degli Avignonesi 22; tel: 06-481 7538; Tue–Sat 12.45–2.45pm, 7.45–10.45pm, Sun 7.45–10.45pm; map F2

Relive *Roman Holiday* or *La Dolce Vita* on a **walk** through Rome's **iconic film locations**

From 1940s neo-realism to the latest pop culture, Rome is one of the silver screen's prized backdrops. You can follow in the footsteps of a number of film icons in a relaxing stroll from Piazza del Popolo to the Trevi Fountain.

Slip on your sunglasses at Piazza del Popolo for a bit of *La Dolce Vita*, where Marcello Mastroianni and Anouk Aimée had their late-night tête-à-tête in Fellini's 1960 film. Head south down the high-end shopping street, Via del Babuino, and turn left on Via Margutta. Originally a bohemian enclave where Fellini and other artists lived, the Via Margutta is a coveted address for the wealthy, lined with private residences, galleries and shops. Poke your head into 52, if the doorman allows – this is where reporter Joe Bradley (Gregory Peck) brings a tipsy Princess Ann (Audrey Hepburn) home in *Roman Holiday* (1953).

Follow Via Margutta to its end, turn right and then immediately left back onto Via del Babuino to Piazza di Spagna. Imagine the fictitious Caffè Dinelli where the nefarious Tom Ripley (Matt Damon) reads a newspaper in 1999's *The Talented Mr Ripley*, or grab an ice cream at the bottom of the Spanish Steps like Audrey Hepburn in *Roman Holiday*.

Walk down Via Due Macelli on the far left and cross Via del Tritone. Desperately look into the tunnel at Via Traforo as Antonio did in Vittorio de Sica's neo-realist masterpiece *The Bicycle Thief* (1948). Turn right and head south on Via Scuderie, which leads to the Trevi Fountain where you can envisage Hepburn and her newly cut pixie hair in *Roman Holiday*, or bathing beauty Anita Ekberg on her *La Dolce Vita* moonlight dip. Finish by tossing your spare pennies in the fountain, like the three gals in 1954's *Three Coins in a Fountain*.

Begin at Piazza del Popolo; map C5

Glam it up with cocktails and caviar at the sophisticated **Hotel de Russie**

'French mojitos', a garden brunch, a butterfly oasis and a world-renowned sommelier... it is not surprising that the Hotel de Russie is castle and court to the world's glamorous and celebrity jet set. On any sunny day, or starry evening, the extensive terraced gardens in the Russie's courtyard are filled with chatter of the beautifully dressed and sun-glassed guests and visitors to the **Jardin de Russie**.

This outdoor restaurant, which has an admirable brunch, lunch and dinner menu, has as its backdrop a butterfly garden. It is often best to reserve in advance, especially for the highly anticipated weekend brunch, which never disappoints, with a creative and abundant selection, and a who's who of guests.

For a sneak peek at *la vie en rose*, plan a sunset visit to the Russie's **Stravinskij Bar**. Its menu of light fare is a less expensive alternative to the restaurant, with artistic cocktails complemented by inimitable hors d'œuvre, such as the De Russie Martini served with caviar or the elusive French mojito and delicious sweet potato chips.

The early evening, from 7.15pm, is the witching hour for the Stravinskij Bar, so dress accordingly.

If people-watching is not on your menu, but you still hunger for an afternoon of personal glam, the Hotel de Russie's **Wellness Zone** should touch the right spots with treatments such as the Four Hands ritual, a simultaneous head, body and foot massage that lasts for nearly two hours.

Hotel de Russie; via del Babuino 9; tel: 06-328 881; www.hotelderussie.it; map C5

Send a postcard home in 14th-century splendour at the delightful **San Silvestro Post Office**

Rome's main post office, Posta Centrale, makes the sending of postcards an unexpectedly rewarding and relaxing experience.

Located on the ground floor of a 14th-century convent, Posta Centrale occupies the inner walls of the former cloister. The original courtyard has been maintained and has lovely foliage and flowers. The atrium is enclosed by glass, illuminating the ceiling and wall decorations of Renaissance frescoes, bas- reliefs and architectural ornaments.

Visitors take a number for the desired service, such as the purchase of stamps *(francobolli)*, and they can then relax in comfortable seating until their number is called.

There is also a charming post office shop to browse, which sells envelopes, books, stationery, videos and gifts – an Italian post box that doubles as a piggy bank is a typical souvenir.

Poste Italiane, the Italian postal service, is not always the most speedy, especially in August. For that reason, many prefer to mail their postcards from the ever-reliable **Poste Vaticane**, the Vatican's post office, just across the river in the Piazza San Pietro *(p.70)*. But bear in mind that each service has its own stamps, and one is not recognised by the other.

Posta Centrale; Piazza San Silvestro 19; Mon–Fri 8am–7pm, Sat 8am–1.15pm; map E3

Join the policemen and politicians for a taste of quintessential **Roman *gelato* at Giolitti**

Tucked away on a nondescript side street near the Pantheon is another temple of worship, to one of Italy's most sacred and delectable treasures: *gelato*.

Beneath a huge neon 'Giolitti' sign is the entrance to this sweet paradise. The city's most famous *gelateria artigianale* has long been a favourite of the fashionable, as well as policemen and politicians – the Italian parliament is just down the road in the Piazza di Montecitorio.

The Giolitti family has been serving up scoops since 1900 when Nazzareno and his wife Giuseppina expanded the family creamery. More than a hundred years later, they have more flavours than years in business. Try the Champagne with a bit of *pompelmo* (grapefruit) for a refreshing summertime treat, or experiment with *riso i pistacchio* (rice and pistachio).

For a true once-in-a-lifetime sundae experience, try the classic Coppa Giolitti (chocolate, cream, zabaglione, with whipped cream), or a delicious dish celebrating a sporting event, such as the Coppa Olimpica, created in honour of the 1960 summer Games held in Rome, and the Coppa Mondiale, which continues to celebrate Italy's hosting of the 1990 World Cup.

For the rare curmudgeon who shuns ice cream, a selection of pastries and cakes along with a Roman *caffè* should please anyone who has even a sliver of sweet in their tooth.

Other nearby favourite ice-cream parlours are **Il Gelato di San Crispino** (Via della Panetteria 42; off map area), which sells ice cream in tubs with seasonal flavours, and the **Gelateria al Teatro** *(p.30)*.

Giolitti; Via Uffici del Vicario 40; tel: 06-699 1243; www.giolitti.it; daily 7am–1.30am; map D2

The Vatican, Borgo and Prati

- Aula delle Udienze Pontificie **C2**
- Basilica di San Pietro **C2**
- Cantina Tirolese **F3**
- Cappella Sistina (Sistine Chapel) **C2**
- Castel Sant'Angelo & Passetto Lungotevere Castello **G3**
- Fontana della Palle di Canone (Fountain of the Cannonballs) **F3**
- Fontana dell' Acqua Angelica (Angelic Water Fountain) **E3**
- Franchi **F4**
- Hotel Cavalieri - Hilton **C4**
- Hotel Columbus **E2**
- Il Matriciano **E4**
- Largo del Colonnato (Fountain of Tiaras) **D3**
- Largo di Porta Castello **F3**
- Mausoleo di Adriano **G2**
- Mercato **E4**
- Musei Vaticani (Vatican Museums) **C4**
- Office of the Prefettura **D2**
- Ospedale Santo Spirito (Santo Spirito Complex) **E2**
- Palazzo del Sant' Uffizio **D2**
- Palazzo della Rovere **E2**
- Palazzo Giraud **E2**
- Piazza Americo Capponi **E3**
- Piazza del Catalone **E3**
- Piazza del Risorgimento **D4**
- Piazza della Vaschette **E3**
- Piazza Giovanni XXIII **F2**
- Piazza Pia **F3**
- Piazza Pio XII **E2**
- Piazza San Pietro (St Peters Square) **D2**
- Porta Cavalleggeri **D2**
- Porta S. Spirito **E1**
- Residenza Paolo VI **D2**
- Scavi Grottoes (Bone Church) **C2**
- Sistine Chapel (Cappella Sistina) **C2**
- St Peters Square (Piazza San Pietro) **D2**
- Teatro Adriano **G4**
- Via di Conciliazione **E2**

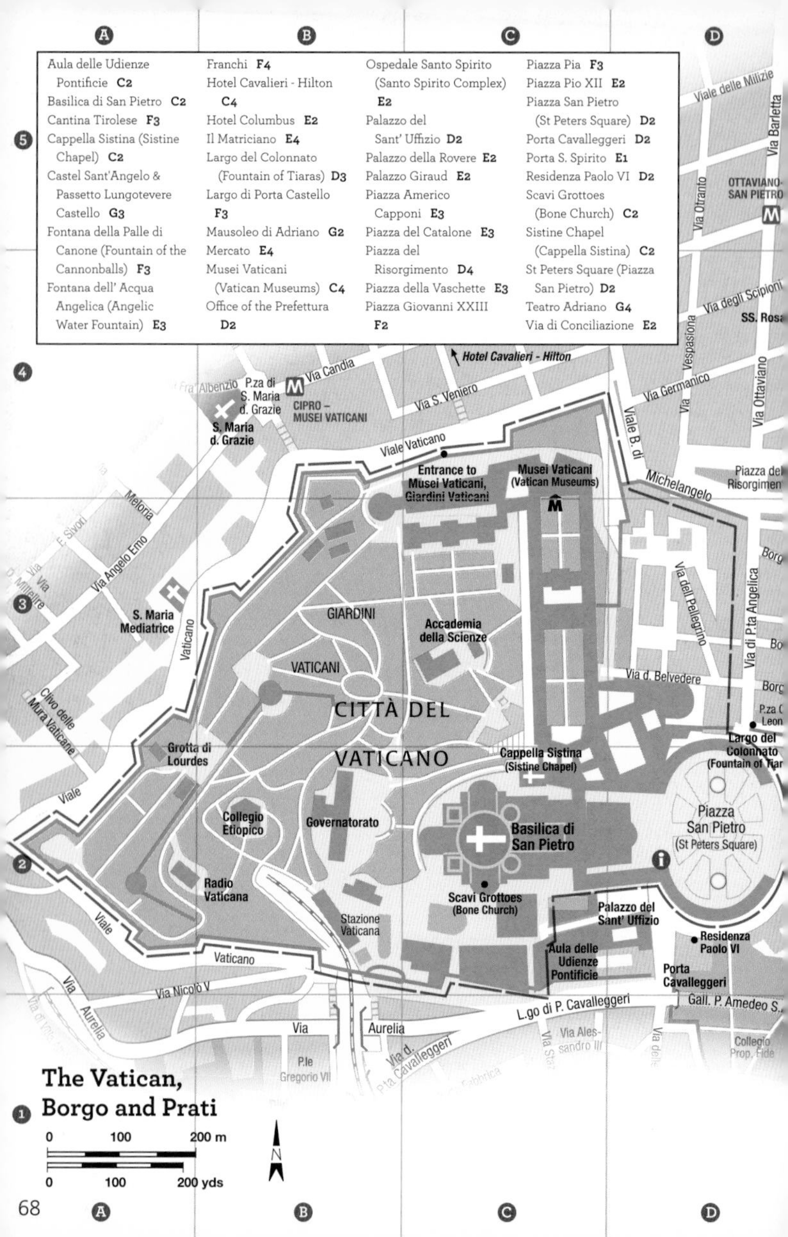

The Vatican, Borgo and Prati

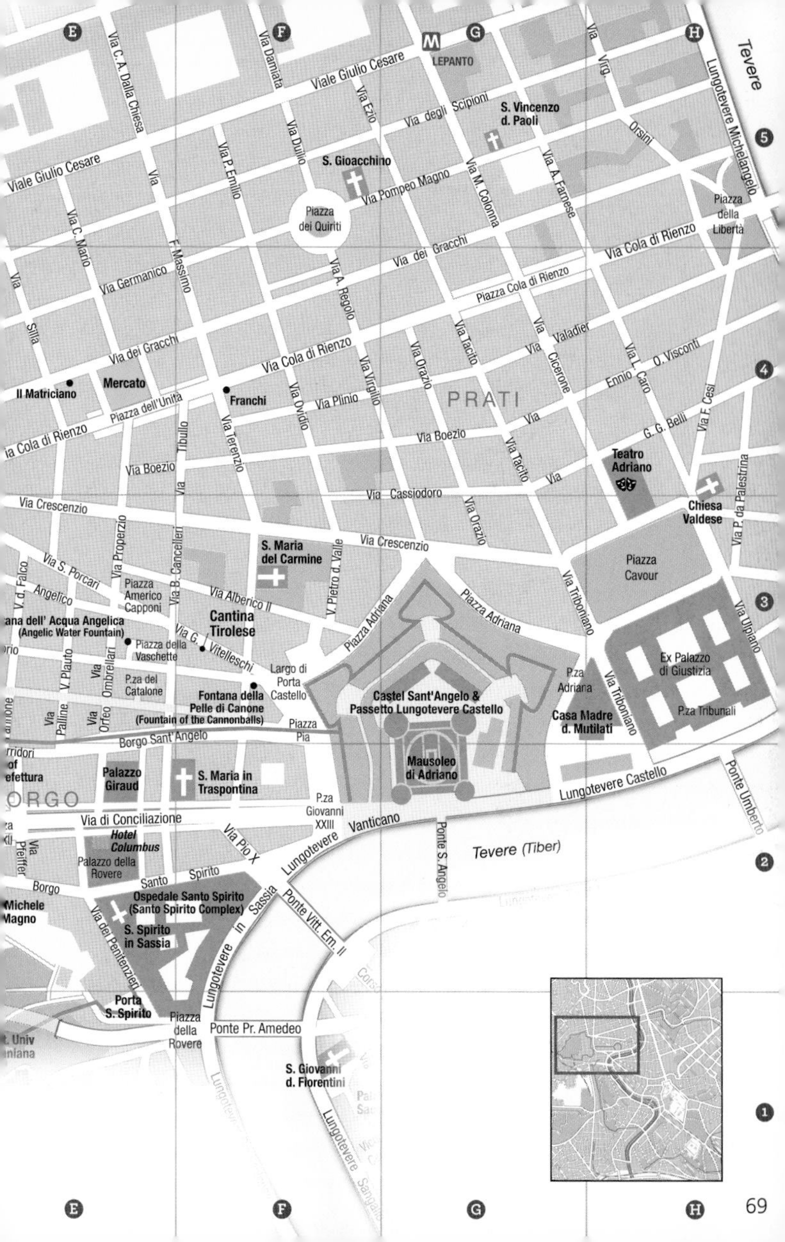
E
F
G
H
LEPANTO
Tevere
Viale Giulio Cesare
Via C. A. Dalla Chiesa
Via Damiata
Via Ezio
Via degli Scipioni
S. Vincenzo d. Paoli
Via Virg.
Orsini
Lungotevere Michelangelo
5
Via Duilio
S. Gioacchino
Via Pompeo Magno
Piazza dei Quiriti
Via P. Emilio
Via M. Colonna
Via A. Farnese
Piazza della Libertà
Via Cola di Rienzo
Via C. Mario
Via F. Massimo
Via Germanico
Via dei Gracchi
Via A. Regolo
Piazza Cola di Rienzo
Via Silla
Via Tacito
Via Valadier
Via Cicerone
Via L. Caro
O. Visconti
Ennio
4
Via dei Gracchi
Via Cola di Rienzo
Via Orazio
Via Virgilio
Via Ovidio
Il Matriciano
Mercato
Franchi
Via Plinio
PRATI
Via F. Cesi
Piazza dell'Unità
Via G. G. Belli
Via Cola di Rienzo
Via Tibullo
Via Terenzio
Via Boezio
Via Boezio
Via Tacito
Teatro Adriano
Via Cassiodoro
Via Orazio
Chiesa Valdese
Via P. da Palestrina
Via Crescenzio
Via Properzio
Via B. Cancellieri
S. Maria del Carmine
V. Pietro d. Valle
Via Crescenzio
Piazza Cavour
Via V. d. Falco
Via S. Porcari
Angelico
Piazza Americo Capponi
Via Alberico II
Via Triboniano
3
Fontana dell' Acqua Angelica
(Angelic Water Fountain)
Cantina Tirolese
Piazza Adriana
Piazza Adriana
Via Ulpiano
Piazza della Vaschette
Via G. Vitelleschi
V. Plauto
Via Ombrellari
P.za del Catalone
Largo di Porta Castello
P.za Adriana
Via Triboniano
Ex Palazzo di Giustizia
Fontana della Pelle di Canone
(Fountain of the Cannonballs)
Castel Sant'Angelo &
Passetto Lungotevere Castello
Via Palline
Via Orfeo
Piazza Pia
Casa Madre d. Mutilati
P.za Tribunali
Borgo Sant'Angelo
Palazzo Giraud
S. Maria in Traspontina
Mausoleo di Adriano
Ponte Umberto
Lungotevere Castello
P.za Giovanni XXIII
Via di Conciliazione
Hotel Columbus
Lungotevere Vanticano
Via Pio X
Ponte S. Angelo
Tevere (Tiber)
Via Pfeiffer
Palazzo della Rovere
Borgo Santo Spirito
2
Ospedale Santo Spirito
(Santo Spirito Complex)
Lungotevere in Sassia
Ponte Vitt. Em. II
Michele Magno
Via dei Penitenzieri
S. Spirito in Sassia
Porta S. Spirito
Piazza della Rovere
Ponte Pr. Amedeo
S. Giovanni d. Fiorentini
1
Lungotevere Sangallo
E
F
G
H

Join the devout in **St Peter's Square** for an **audience with the Pope**

Twice a week Piazza San Pietro fills with thousands of Roman Catholics coming to hear the Pope give his blessing. This giant eliptical square was added in 1656 during the final phase of decoration of the new basilica. Gianlorenzo Bernini was commissioned by Pope Alexander VII to create a space that reflected the role of the church. The floor plan is shaped like a giant keyhole, reinforcing the role of St Peter as heaven's gatekeeper. High above the colonnade, which half encircles an Egyptian obelisk brought here in AD 37, are more than 200 colossal statues of saints.

On Wednesdays from September to June Pope Benedict XIV holds court at 10.30am in the piazza (in Nervi Hall during inclement weather). Visitors must request tickets in advance from the Office of the Prefettura della Casa Ponteficia (or simply watch from afar on giant TV screens). These audiences are conducted in Italian, French, English, German, Croatian, Portuguese and Spanish. Cheering, dancing and singing, almost anything goes, as long as it's not in bad taste.

On Sundays at noon, Piazza San Pietro swells for the Angelus service when the Pope gives a blessing from an upper window.

Piazza San Pietro; Wed 10.30am; map D2; write to Prefettura della Casa Pontificia, 00120 Città del Vaticano; fax: 06-6988-5378; or go in person Mon, Tue 9am–1pm

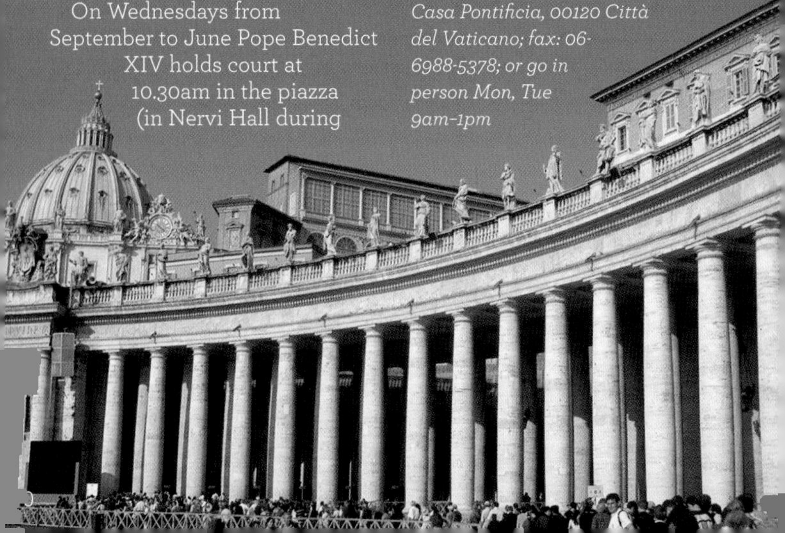

Dip into a fondue in a small corner of Alpine Austria at the **Pope's favourite restaurant**

When you visit **Cantina Tirolese**, keep your eyes open for table six where a placard in Italian reads: 'We've lost a wonderful client but gained a great Pope.'

This was a favourite haunt of Cardinal Ratzinger before he became Benedict XIV. Born in Munich, he enjoyed home cooking from his mother who was from South Tyrol.

A little bit of Alpine Austria on the edge of the Borgo, the Cantina Tirolese seems far from Rome. Wooden benches, beer steins and colourful cloth banners decorate the cosy ground-level dining area, and the cantina is much the same, with long banquet tables. The vibe is vintage Austrian – only the Italian-speaking staff seems out of place.

Bourguignonne (beef cooked in oil) was a favourite of Cardinal Ratzinger, as was Spalenbraus beer and Sachertorte. The meat selection is heavy with familiar fillets, Wiener schnitzel, Viennese goulash, beef stroganoff, Asiatique (beef cooked in broth), and specialities like Ghiottone Grill, a selection of meats grilled at the table. There is a range of cheeses for the fondue, and to drink there is a thorough selection of beers on tap and in bottles.

Alternatively, for a simple, traditional Roman meal, just a stone's throw away from the Vatican walls and near Piazza Risorgimento, try **Il Matriciano** (Via dei Gracchi 55; tel: 06-321 2327; closed Wed in winter, Sat in summer; map E4). A speciality is *bucatini all'amatriciana*, thick, hollow spaghetti with tomato, bacon and pecorino cheese.

Cantina Tirolese; Via Vitelleschi 23; tel: 06-6813 5297; www.cantinatirolese.it; Tue–Sun noon–midnight; map F3

Sidestep the crowds at the **Vatican Museums** to discover **beautiful frescoes in the Pinacoteca**

A visit to the Vatican Museums requires both patience and perseverance. It is the most visited location in Rome, and to sidestep the crowds and enjoy these extensive themed galleries, it helps to know where you are going and what you want to see. A wonderful spiral ramp *(pictured)* designed by Giuseppe Momo leads up to the admissions area where small television screens show which galleries are open.

From the start, avoid the masses, who immediately migrate towards the Sistine Chapel at the far end of the galleries. Head instead for the nearby **Pinacoteca**, the 'new' art gallery wing. It was built in 1932 to display 460 of the pope's most prestigious works of art including such famous paintings as Giotto's *Stefaneschi Triptych*, Raphael's *Madonna of Foligno* and *Transfiguration*, Leonardo's *Saint Jerome* and Caravaggio's *Entombment*.

Take your time in Sala IV, a room dedicated to the frescoes of Melozzo da Forlì. These late 15th-century frescoes were painted directly on the walls of two Roman churches, eventually removed and displayed on the Pinacoteca walls. Beautiful fragments hang along a curved wall depicting gorgeous angels and heads of Apollo. The large adjacent Sistus IV panel shows Forlì's foreshortening flair.

From the Pinacoteca head towards the **Cortile della Pigna**, a late Renaissance courtyard named after the 1st-century AD large bronze pine cone in the main niche. From here you can enjoy a stroll through the many galleries that line the courtyards.

Beside the Cortile della Pigna is the **Chiaramonti Museum** in the Braccio Nuovo (New Wing) where among the ancient statuary you will find the Augustus of Prima Porta – a 2m-high, detailed statue of the Emperor from the

TACKLING THE MUSEUMS

The best advice for a visit to the museum is to prepare. The Vatican website, www.vatican.va, describes every gallery and nearly every work of art, and allows purchase of timed-entrance tickets for morning as well as evening visits (7–9.30pm). The museums also offer multilingual and detailed audioguides, the English-language version recorded by a British art historian. In addition, many tour companies, such as **Context Travel** (www.contexttravel.com/rome), offer private visits and special entrances led by acclaimed scholars.

1st century BC. The gallery leads to the **Scala di Bramante**, Donato Bramante's exposed spiral staircase behind the Octagonal courtyard, with a fabulously detailed herringbone floor and a spectacular view of Rome.

Finally, it is worth navigating the bottleneck at the far end of the galleries, past four impressive Raphael rooms decorated by the artist and his school (including *The School of Athens; pictured p.66*), to reach the **Niccoline Chapel**. Rarely open, this room is a jewel box, glowing from lapis-lazuli vaulting pricked with gold stars, and covered with rich frescoes by Fra Angelico (1450).

Musei Vaticani; Viale Vaticano 100; tel: 06-6988 4947; www.vatican.va; Mon–Sat, 9am–6pm, last entry 4pm; charge, free last Sun of month; map C4

Experience the majestic **St Peter's Basilica** from the lofty dome to the subterranean necropolis

If the 360-degree view from Michelangelo's **dome** of the Basilica di San Pietro is divine, the climb to the top is a true test of faith. From the basilica floor to the tip of its gold cross, St Peter's dome is the tallest in the world at 136.5m. The dedicated few climb more than 500 steps to the top, while the rest take a lift to the terrace roof, leaving a further 320-stair climb. For a more relaxing experience, linger on the terrace below the cupola with a view of the Piazza San Pietro.

Michelangelo was just one of the architects involved in building St Peter's, which was consecrated in 1626. Bramante, Raphael and Maderno were also employed in the 120-year project.

The basilica was built on the foundation of a 4th-century church, which in turn was built on a Roman necropolis. The **grottoes**, immediately below the basilica floor, house the tombs of the popes, including John Paul II.

The Vatican **necropolis** on the second level beneath the basilica's floor, is the most holy area of Vatican City. The Scavi is an excavation of a 1st-century BC burial ground that includes the tomb of St Peter, founder of the Christian church. The 90-minute guided walk in the necropolis is available to only 200 selected people each day. Requests must be made at least 90 days in advance.

Basilica di San Pietro, map C2; dome: Apr–Sept 8am–6pm, Oct–Mar 8am–4.45pm, charge; grottoes: Apr–Sept 7am–6pm, Oct–Mar 7am–5pm, free; necropolis: Ufficio Scavi, 00120 Città del Vatican, tel: 06-6988 5318, fax: 06-6987 3017, email scavi@fsp.va

Indulge yourself at the exclusive **La Pergola**, Rome's only **three-Michelin-starred restaurant**

Luxury in Rome is not hard to come by, but exclusivity is. Set apart from the buzz of the city is the Hotel Cavalieri, high on the Montemario hill. And on its rooftop precipice, overlooking the cityscape, is La Pergola, the most sought-after restaurant in Rome.

La Pergola is the Eternal City's only Michelin three-star restaurant and one of six in the entire country. Chef Heinz Beck unleashes fierce imagination in his dishes of creative Italian cuisine. The signature tasting menu of nine dishes (just under €200), changes seasonally, and the grand dessert is an ultra-modern confection that has earned the epithet 'Beckian'. The experience is both impeccable and unforgettable. Guests gaze out at the sparkling city while choosing from 29 spring and mountain waters. Waiters attend to every beck and call, and wine comes from a 3,000-label cellar.

If the restaurant is a little too exclusive but you want to enjoy the hotel's luxury, try a designer hamburger at the Pool Bar or an afternoon of pampering at the Grand Spa. And don't miss the art-works, including a monumental canvas by Tiepolo.

La Pergola, Hotel Rome Cavalieri; Via Cadlolo 101; tel: 06-3509 2152; www.romecavalieri.com; Tue–Sat 7.30–11.30pm; map C4

ROME'S MICHELIN STARS

Notables include **Il Pagliaccio** (Via dei Banchi Vecchi 129; tel: 06-6880 9595; map p.24 C3) with two stars; and with one: **Agata e Romeo** (Via Carlo Alberto 45; tel: 06-446 6115; off map area), **Glass Hostaria** (Vicolo del Cinque 58; tel: 06-5833 5903; map p.103 E3), **Baby** at the Aldrovandi Hotel *(p.78)*, **Imàgo** *(p.127)*, **Mirabelle** *(p.127)* and **Open Colonna** *(p.149)*.

Savour spectacular **sunset views** and sip on summer cocktails at the **Castel Sant'Angelo**

When your afternoon is winding down, head over to Castel Sant'Angelo and wind your way up to the Terrazza dell'Angelo, a wide-open platform on top of the fort. At this vantage point, standing below a bronze angel, you can watch the setting sun paint the rooftops of Rome red, from the chariots on the Altare della Patria to the dome of St Peter's Basilica.

Castel Sant'Angelo is a medieval papal stronghold, built on the 2nd-century AD cylindrical Mausoleum of the Emperor Hadrian. It was originally topped with cypress trees and lavishly decorated, and colossal statuary fragments are visible at the entrance. Walk down a helical ramp to the main burial chamber at the centre of the rotunda, then head up the spiral to the top to capture Rome's resplendent panorama.

As you make your way down, stop at the 4th floor and walk around the outer rim. Here among 2nd-century statue fragments is a life-size marble bust of Hadrian. Continue west to the café for a view of St Peter's dome while sipping Prosecco, and reflecting that it was from here that Puccini's Tosca plunged to her death.

From June to August Il Passetto di Borgo, the medieval corridor and papal escape route connecting Castel Sant'Angelo with the Vatican, opens for evening strolls, while the bastions of the surrounding medieval wall turn into a nightspot with cocktails, music and tomfoolery at a summertime restaurant and bar.

Castel Sant'Angelo; Lungotevere Castello 50; tel: 06-681 911; www.museocastelsantangelo.com; Tue–Sun 9am–7pm; charge; map G2

Enjoy nature with a quiet walk through the formal **Vatican Gardens**

The Vatican has the most meditative lawns in Rome, but unlike public parks such as Villa Borghese or Villa Pamphilj, there is a dress code at the Vatican Gardens and they are only accessible to those who reserve a guided visit.

The garden tour follows a path through 23 hectares of flowerbeds, topiary, woodland, medieval fortifications, buildings and monuments. And though you cannot freely meander along the paths, this guided walk among coiffed lawns and box hedges is always inspiring.

The gardens were conceived in the 13th century under Pope Nicholas III. After moving the papal residence back to the Vatican from the Lateran Palace, he wanted a garden for his personal use. He planted an orchard, lawn and beds, which subsequent popes would redesign and redevelop, adding sculptures, grottoes and buildings.

The recently restored medieval St John's Tower on the western hilltop next to the papal helipad is reserved for illustrious guests. Nearby is the 94m-high aerial tower for Vatican Radio, 'The voice of the Pope' transmitted in 47 languages as part of the Vatican's radio and television broadcasting organisation.

Villa Pia, towards the end of the tour, is a high Mannerist villa with ornaments and fountains. Built as a relaxation spot for the pope, his emissaries and guests, it is now the seat of the Pontifical Academy of Sciences and their yearly congresses.

The garden tour ends with entry into the Vatican Museums and Sistine Chapel.

Vatican Gardens; Viale Vaticano; www.biglietteriamusei.vatican.va; Mon–Sat; online reservations required; charge; map B3

Cycle along the banks of the Tiber from Castel Sant'Angelo to the Milvian Bridge

Although Rome was built on seven hills, the neighbourhoods around the centre are on flat ground ideal for the urban biker. The perfect ride, however, isn't on Rome's streets – it is below on the south bank of the River Tiber. The path of choice is a 4.5km ride from Ponte Cavour (map p.46 C3) to Ponte Milvio (map p.122 C5), an easy 25 minutes along the Tiber, which includes three uphill and two downhill ramps.

Biking along the Tiber isn't limited to the Cavour–Milvio trail. Every staircase to the Tiber banks, located next to each bridge, has a bike rail to place your wheels so you can push your bike up or down. Ponte Matteotti, connecting Prati and Popolo, has a wide ramp (west side) for easy ascents and descents.

The best bike rental is in Campo de' Fiori at **Collalti** (Via del Pellegrino 82; tel: 06-6880 1084; map p.24 C3). **Roma Bike Sharing** (www.roma-n-bike.com) has short-term rentals for subscribers, with stations in Prati and Ponte Sant'Angelo. The scheme has 300 bicycles in 25 locations.

Roma Bike Tour (www.romabiketour.com) offers tours on folding Brompton bikes, from Vatican City to Ponte Milvio and back to the centre, in English, French and Italian.

PONTE MILVIO BARS

Stick around for *aperitivo* hour at Piazzale Ponte Milvio (map p.122 B–C5). **Il Chioschetto**, on the bridge and open in balmy months, and **Caffè Ponte Milvio** (Piazzale Ponte Milvio 44) are king and queen of the scene with delicious snacks to accompany your drinks. Newcomers, such as *sandwicherie* **Aristocampo** (34), tiny wine bar **Jarro** at (32) and, around the corner on Via Flaminia, **Voy** (496) with live jazz, and tapas-serving **Diagonal** (490), are catching up.

See the riches of the **12th-century Santo Spirito hospital**, refuge for abandoned babies

Most museums are closed on Mondays, which gives you the opportunity to pass an hour in the medieval hospital of Santo Spirito in Saxia. It was started in the 8th century as a pilgrim refuge, and in the 12th century enlarged under Pope Innocent III who decreed it should help the sick, the poor and the *proietti*, abandoned and illegitimate babies.

It is Rome's oldest and most decorative hospital. The impressive Corsia Sistina (Sistine Ward) is the high point. The 120m-long colonnaded hallway has traces of frescoes depicting the history of the hospital, including its 15th-century rebuilding under its patron Pope Sixtus IV, who also gave his name to the Sistine Chapel. Stand at its centre and look up at the richly decorated *tiburio*, an octagonal dome with frescoes and the Pope's family crests, and then take in the marble altar, a rare example of Andrea Palladio's architecture in Rome.

The multi-building complex also contains the Accademia Lancisiana, an 18th-century library with some 17,000 volumes, and the Palazzo del Commendatore (palace of the hospital director), a multi-levelled palace with tapered arches, a Baroque clock tower and central fountain. In the middle of the complex is the Museo dell'Arte Sanitaria, with medicine and surgical items.

When you leave at the Borgo Santo Spirito entrance, look immediately to your right. Sticking out from the wall is a small vestibule with curved grill where mothers and nursemaids gave up their babies to the care of the church.

Santo Spirito Complex; Borgo Santo Spirito 1; tel 06-6835 2433; www.giubilarte.it; tours Mon 10am, 3.30pm; charge; map E2

Stock up on cheese and **top-quality prosciutto** at the **Cola di Rienzo indoor market**

Rome reinvented the neighbourhood market *(mercato rionale)* in the mid-1920s, building indoor emporia stocked with produce from the local Lazio region. They are still the first choice of Roman shoppers, who can hand-pick vegetables, fruits, cheeses, fish and meat.

At Piazza dell'Unità, on Via Cola di Rienzo, is a neoclassical white and pale yellow building, with the sign 'Mercato Rionale' above the entrance. Here you can stock your picnic basket, have your shoes shined at the *calzolaio* or pick up any number of Italian treats to take home.

The vegetable stand immediately on the left of the entrance always draws a crowd for its fresh produce. Look for stand 32, a popular *salumeria*, with prosciutto, *bresaola*, salami and other cured meats, as well as cheese. Stand 31 sells Garofalo, prestigious dried pasta from Naples, and home-made gnocchi and tortellini. Nearby are two *casalinghi* shops selling homeware, cleaning items and knick-knacks. Spend time making small talk and you may learn the secrets of stain removal.

Mercato Rionale; Piazza dell'Unità, corner Via Properzio and Via Cola di Rienzo; Mon–Sat 9am–5pm; map E4

A STAND-OUT STAND-UP

Franchi Gastronomia (Via Cola di Rienzo 204; tel: 06-687 4651; Mon–Sat 9am–7pm; map F4) is an historic gourmet deli where patrons stand in chic overcoats to nibble the day's delicacies. The counter has salamis and cheeses, as well as prepared dishes like salmon filet, fresh octopus salad, roast veal and Roman artichokes – all available for eating at their bar corner or packed to take away. Not to miss here are their famed *suppli*, ragu- and mozzarella-stuffed rice balls, which Romans have consistently ranked as the top *suppli* in the entire city.

Seek out papal fountains in a walk through the medieval **Borgo neighbourhood**

Wherever you see a coat of arms with the crossed keys of St Peter topped with the *triregnum* triple crown, you know the building, sculpture or painting on which it appears was a papal commission. Meandering through the quaint streets of the medieval Borgo neighbourhood, which has a lion on its own coat of arms, you can seek out papal family crests, too.

Start out at Largo del Colonnato on the north side of Piazza San Pietro. Just outside the colonnade, the three-tiered **Fontana delle Tiare** (Fountain of Tiaras; map D2) shows off the papal crest. Follow the wall along Via dei Corridori, turning left under the archway at Via del Mascherino. Above you is the Medici crest, six balls in a circle. Medici pope Leo X brought the Borgo to its heyday in the early 16th century by entertaining guests in the neighbourhood.

Turn immediately right on Borgo Pio, left on Via degli Ombrellari, then right on Borgo Vittorio. Recessed into the pavement of Piazza delle Vaschette is the **Fontana dell'Acqua Angelica** (Fountain of Angelic Water; map E3), said to have healing waters.

Across the street at the end of Borgo Vittorio is the **Fontana delle Palle di Canone** (Fountain of the Cannonballs; map F3) bearing the Borgo arms. Head back on Borgo Pio, and look for the ivy-covered building at Piazza del Catalone. In the foreground is the red-brick **Fontana del Catalone** (map F3) with the papal tiara and keys.

Turn right on Vicolo del Campanile, which leads to the modern Via della Conciliazione. Though this area was redesigned in 1928, the architects simply reoriented the early Renaissance palazzi. Across the street, at 33, is the late 15th-century Palazzo della Rovere, with the oak tree crest of della Rovere pope Sistus IV. On the Palazzo della Rovere's facade is the **Fontana del Borgo Vecchio** (*pictured*; map E2). Take a sip of water from the lips of the dragon on the Borgo's favourite fountain.

Colosseo and Celio

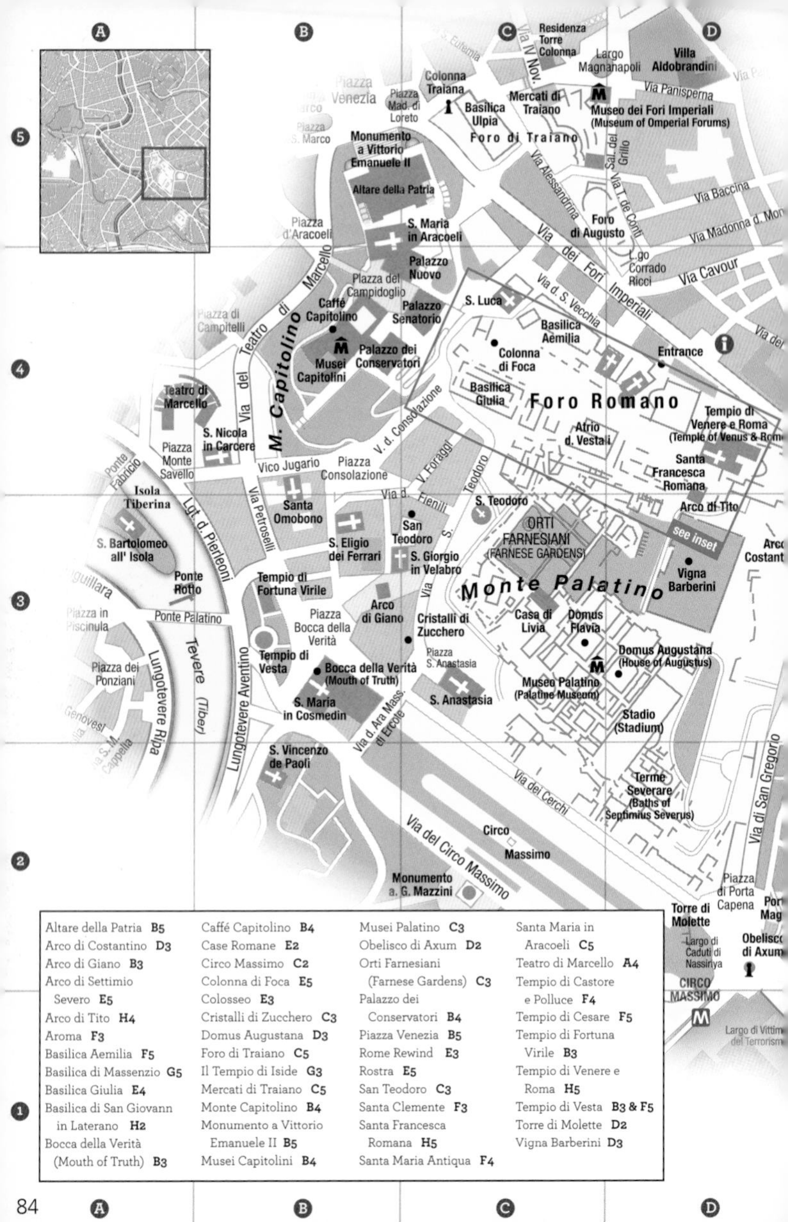

Altare della Patria **B5**
Arco di Costantino **D3**
Arco di Giano **B3**
Arco di Settimio Severo **E5**
Arco di Tito **H4**
Aroma **F3**
Basilica Aemilia **F5**
Basilica di Massenzio **G5**
Basilica Giulia **E4**
Basilica di San Giovann in Laterano **H2**
Bocca della Verità (Mouth of Truth) **B3**
Caffé Capitolino **B4**
Case Romane **E2**
Circo Massimo **C2**
Colonna di Foca **E5**
Colosseo **E3**
Cristalli di Zucchero **C3**
Domus Augustana **D3**
Foro di Traiano **C5**
Il Tempio di Iside **G3**
Mercati di Traiano **C5**
Monte Capitolino **B4**
Monumento a Vittorio Emanuele II **B5**
Musei Capitolini **B4**
Musei Palatino **C3**
Obelisco di Axum **D2**
Orti Farnesiani (Farnese Gardens) **C3**
Palazzo dei Conservatori **B4**
Piazza Venezia **B5**
Rome Rewind **E3**
Rostra **E5**
San Teodoro **C3**
Santa Clemente **F3**
Santa Francesca Romana **H5**
Santa Maria Antiqua **F4**
Santa Maria in Aracoeli **C5**
Teatro di Marcello **A4**
Tempio di Castore e Polluce **F4**
Tempio di Cesare **F5**
Tempio di Fortuna Virile **B3**
Tempio di Venere e Roma **H5**
Tempio di Vesta **B3 & F5**
Torre di Molette **D2**
Vigna Barberini **D3**

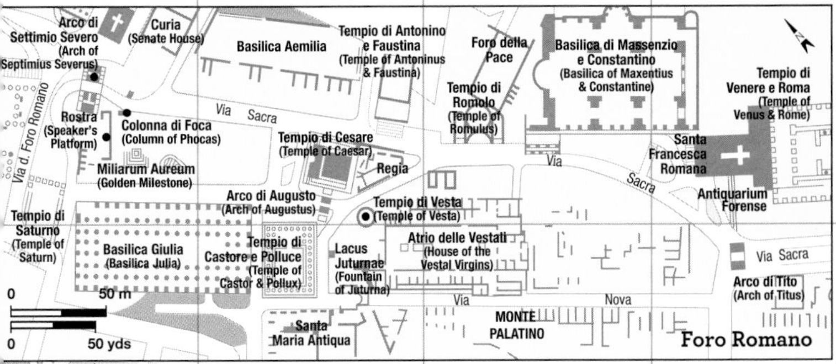
E
F
G
H
Arco di Settimio Severo (Arch of Septimius Severus)
Curia (Senate House)
Basilica Aemilia
Tempio di Antonino e Faustina (Temple of Antoninus & Faustina)
Foro della Pace
Basilica di Massenzio e Constantino (Basilica of Maxentius & Constantine)
Tempio di Venere e Roma (Temple of Venus & Rome)
Tempio di Romolo (Temple of Romulus)
Via Sacra
Rostra (Speaker's Platform)
Colonna di Foca (Column of Phocas)
Tempio di Cesare (Temple of Caesar)
Regia
Santa Francesca Romana
Via d. Foro Romano
Miliarum Aureum (Golden Milestone)
Arco di Augusto (Arch of Augustus)
Tempio di Vesta (Temple of Vesta)
Antiquarium Forense
Tempio di Saturno (Temple of Saturn)
Basilica Giulia (Basilica Julia)
Tempio di Castore e Polluce (Temple of Castor & Pollux)
Lacus Juturnae (Fountain of Juturna)
Atrio delle Vestali (House of the Vestal Virgins)
Via Sacra
Arco di Tito (Arch of Titus)
Via Nova
0
50 m
0
50 yds
Santa Maria Antiqua
MONTE PALATINO
Foro Romano
5
4

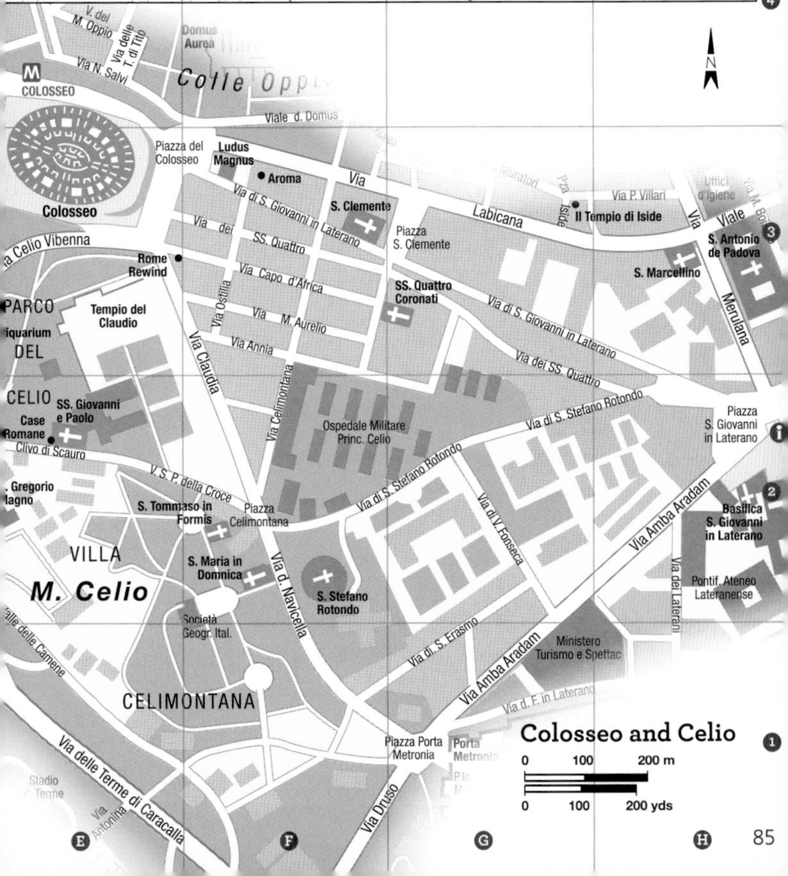
V. del M. Oppio
Via delle T. di Tito
Domus Aurea
Via N. Salvi
COLOSSEO
Colle Oppio
Viale d. Domus Aurea
Piazza del Colosseo
Ludus Magnus
Aroma
Via Labicana
Via Muratori
Pza Iside
Via P. Villari
Uffici d'Igiene
Via M. Boiardo
Colosseo
Via di S. Giovanni in Laterano
S. Clemente
Il Tempio di Iside
Viale Manzoni
S. Antonio de Padova
3
Via dei SS. Quattro
Piazza S. Clemente
Via Celio Vibenna
Rome Rewind
Via Capo d'Africa
SS. Quattro Coronati
S. Marcellino
Via Merulana
PARCO
Tempio del Claudio
Via Ostilia
Via M. Aurelio
Via di S. Giovanni in Laterano
Antiquarium
DEL
Via Annia
Via Claudia
Via dei SS. Quattro
CELIO
SS. Giovanni e Paolo
Via Celimontana
Via di S. Stefano Rotondo
Case Romane
Ospedale Militare Princ. Celio
Piazza S. Giovanni in Laterano
Clivo di Scauro
V. S. P. della Croce
Via di S. Stefano Rotondo
S. Gregorio Magno
S. Tommaso in Formis
Piazza Celimontana
Via di V. Fonseca
Via Amba Aradam
2
Basilica S. Giovanni in Laterano
VILLA
S. Maria in Domnica
Via d. Navicella
S. Stefano Rotondo
Via dei Laterani
Pontif. Ateneo Lateranense
M. Celio
Società Geogr. Ital.
Via di S. Erasmo
Viale delle Camene
Ministero Turismo e Spettac.
Via Amba Aradam
CELIMONTANA
Via d. F. in Laterano
Colosseo and Celio
Via delle Terme di Caracalla
Piazza Porta Metronia
Porta Metronia
1
0
100
200 m
0
100
200 yds
Stadio d. Terme
Via Antonina
Via Druso
E
F
G
H

Walk the **Roman Forum's Sacred Way**, the oldest street in Rome

To walk on the **Via Sacra** (Sacred Way) through the Forum is to walk in the footsteps of some of the greatest figures in history. This was the centre of all social, judicial, religious, financial and commercial activity in the Empire. In this congested hub, traitors were executed, emperors triumphed and everyone heeded what the virgins had to say.

On entering the Forum, you immediately step on to Via Sacra, the oldest road in Rome, from the 7th century BC. Before you is the stepped foundation of the **Temple of Julius Caesar** where in 44 BC the slain Caesar was cremated by an emotional mob incited by the speech of Mark Antony made on the **Rostra**, a stage for public speaking at the far end of the square. Beside the Rostra is the early 3rd-century **Arch of Septimius Severus**, the gateway to the Capitoline hill *(p.92)*, where triumphant generals concluded their victory parades.

In front of the Rostra is the **Column of Phocas.** Named after a Byzantine emperor, it was the last monument placed in the Forum, in AD 608. Look for the nearby cylindrical brick **Mundus,** an 8th-century BC conduit to the underworld and symbolic centre of Ancient Rome.

Return down the dirt road and on the far right, behind a tall brick library, is **Santa Maria Antiqua**, with 8th-century Byzantine frescoes preserved under a landslide, restored and now open to visitors.

Past the three columns of the **Temple of Castor and Pollux** is the small, round, reconstructed **Temple of Vesta**, tended to by the Vestal Virgins, Rome's most important priestesses, with their large living complex beside it. Inside burned Rome's eternal flame and sacred objects purportedly brought by Aeneas from Troy.

On the other side of the Via Sacra is the round **Temple of Romulus**, a charming 4th-century building whose doors are intermittently open. Looking down on it is the **church of saints Cosma and Damiano**, with 6th-century mosaics in the apse.

The last monument at the top of Via Sacra is the **church of Santa Francesca Romana**, attached to Emperor Hadrian's massive **Temple of Venus and Rome**. This spanned 1.2 hectares and had a gilded bronze roof. Recently opened to visitors, it has a beautiful view of the Colosseum.

The best time to visit the Forum is just after it opens at 8.30am, or no later than two hours before sunset, when the colourful hues begin to cool down.

Main entrance on Via dei Fori Imperiali (entrances also at Via di San Gregorio 30 and the Colosseo); tel: 06-3996 7700; www.pierreci.it; daily 8.30am–1hr before sunset; charge; tickets valid for two days for Forum, Palatine Hill and Colosseum; see map inset

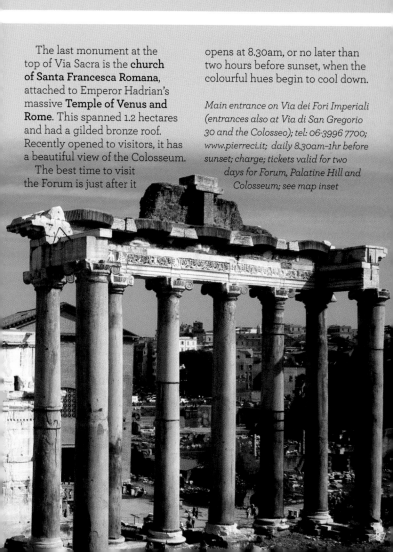

Bask in a **panoramic view of Rome** from the top of the **Altare della Patria**

The Altare della Patria (Altar of the Country) on the northern flank of the Capitoline hill has the most beautiful bird's-eye view of Rome, bar none. The 70m-high ornate white-marble monument may be an eyesore to detractors, who call it the Wedding Cake, but its rooftop **Terrazza delle Quadrighe** has a breathtaking 360-degree view of the city. A special glass elevator delivers visitors to the terrace between the two bronze *quadrighe* (chariot) statues that crown the monument, to see Rome *dal cielo* – from the heavens. The panorama stretches for many kilometres, from the obelisk of Piazza del Popolo, the domes of St Peter's and the Pantheon, the rooftops of Trastevere, around to the treetops of the Roman Forum, Colosseum and Basilica of Maxentius to the neighbourhoods of Esquilino, Quirinale and Via Veneto.

Also called the **Monumento a Vittorio Emanuele II**, this colossal structure commemorates the 1870 Unification and Italy's first king. Not completed until 1935, it contains the Eternal Flame of Rome, the Tomb of the Unknown Soldier, a museum and an imposing 12m statue of the mounted monarch *(pictured)*.

For a drink with a view, pop into the open-air café on the monument's first-level terrace.

Roma dal Cielo, Altare della Patria; entrances at Piazza Aracoeli, Via San Pietro in Carcere and Piazza del Campidoglio; tel: 06-6920 2049; Mon–Thur 9.30am–6.30pm, Fri–Sun 9.30am–7.30pm; charge; map B5

Discover an **ancient Roman shopping mall** at **Trajan's Forum**

MUSEUM OF THE IMPERIAL FORA

Most visitors are often so eager to reach Trajan's marketplace and forum that they ignore this museum housed in the same place they bought their tickets. The glass-enclosed 2nd-century AD brick structure was the most important administrative section of Trajan's markets, which was possibly used for grain distribution to the public. Today it has a state-of-the art museum with a formidable collection of sculpture, along with video and 3-D projections and temporary modern art exhibitions.

Ancient Rome had many conveniences that modern society enjoys, including shopping malls. For a walk through such a building, and to get a feeling of daily life in those days, look for Trajan's Column, standing 38m tall on the east side of Piazza Venezia. Below it was a 24,000 sq metre forum and multistorey shopping experience.

Set out on three terraces in what was once the Quirinal hill, Trajan's Markets were designed by Apollodorus in AD 113 for Emperor Trajan. The upper and lower terraces would have housed offices and provided commercial premises for selling spices, wine, vegetables, oil, seafood, and luxury items such as jewellery. It also had a tavern. Today, visitors roam through the open market rooms, and can visit the partially accessible Trajan's Forum, a massive complex of temples and markets.

Enter the marketplace via the Museum of the Imperial Fora *(see above)* by either walking from Piazza Venezia eastward uphill on Via IV Novembre, or from Piazza Foro Traiano and up the staircase of Via delle Cannelle, turning right onto Via IV November.

Mercato di Traiano and Museo dei Fori Imperiali; Via IV Novembre 94; tel: 060608; www.mercatiditraiano.it; Tue–Sun 9am–7pm; charge; map C5

Pack an **afternoon picnic** for the **Palatine hill** and enjoy a lofty, romantic view of the city

Put together a picnic and head for the hill – the Palatine, where Romulus founded the city, and from where Rome's aristocracy have long taken a lofty view. A green space with remains of numerous palaces, it has also acted as a backdrop for portraits of Grand Tour visitors to the city, and yours will not be the first picnic Prosecco cork to pop here.

The hill rises on the southern edge of the Forum and is part of the visit. From the **Arch of Titus** head south up the ancient Clivus Palatinus to the **Vigna Barberini**, the Barberini family vineyards. This was once a haunt of Romantic writers and painters for its unobstructed view of the Colosseum and the dome of the Temple of Venus.

Settle down for your picnic on the southeastern summit with views of the Circus Maximus. If you need shade, go to the **Farnese Gardens** in the centre of the hill where the terrace gives spectacular views of the heart of Ancient Rome. These pleasure gardens were laid out in the 16th century for the cardinal over the ruins of the Palace of Tiberius.

After lunch, and perhaps a nap, amble through the hill's architectural delights. The **Domus Augustana**, part of the Palatine Museum, may be open; it contains well-preserved 1st-century frescoes. Peruse the remains of the **Domus Flavia**, the house of the Emperor Domitian, who is said to have lined his throne room with mirrors in order to see approaching enemies from any angle. Then walk around 3rd-century Severian arcades.

Palatine hill, Roman Forum; daily 8.30am–1hr before sunset; accessed as part of Forum ticket (p.87); map C3–D3

Test your truthfulness at the **Bocca della Verità**, an ancient lie detector that threatens to bite

Ever since Gregory Peck dared Audrey Hepburn to put her hand in the Mouth of Truth (Bocca della Verità) in the William Wyler classic *Roman Holiday*, visitors have queued at the Church of Santa Maria in Cosmedin to test their probity.

Carved in the 1st century with an open-mouthed human face, the 1300kg round marble mask is thought to have been either part of a fountain or a manhole cover for the Cloaca Maxima, the city's 6th-century BC drainage system. Since the Middle Ages, travellers to Rome have described the Mouth of Truth as a lie detector. Anybody who placed their hand in the mask, and was untruthful or unfaithful, would have it bitten off. Though there is no documentation of unexpected amputations, the Mouth of Truth has amused visitors since it was placed in the portico of Santa Maria in Cosmedin in the 17th century.

Put your hand all the way in. If your test proves successful, take a tour inside the 8th-century church. Its original geometric pavement, re-cut pieces of ancient marble, was inlaid in the 12th century. The central aisle is also an example of medieval recycling, composed of reused ancient columns of disparate marbles.

Across the street are two of the best preserved temples from Republican Rome – the Temple of Portunus and the round Temple of Hercules Olivarius. Though you cannot enter either, walk around the structures to admire the 1st-century BC detail.

Bocca della Verità, church of Santa Maria in Cosmedin; Piazza Bocca della Verità 18; tel: 06-678 1419; map B3

Trace the foundation of Rome at the **Capitoline Museums**

The Capitoline Wolf suckling Rome's founding twins, Romulus and Remus, is an emblem for the city. Though its age is disputed, the bronze sculpture was one of a number donated by Pope Sistus IV in 1471 to the people of Rome, starting what became the first public museum in the world. The Capitoline Museums are in two parts, facing each other across Piazza del Campidoglio: the 15th-century Palazzo dei Conservatori (Conservators' Palace) and Braccio Nuovo (New Wing) completed in 1654.

They occupy the summit of the hill where Rome's largest and most important temple, dating from the 6th century BC, was dedicated to Jupiter, greatest of the gods. A 60m x 60m square section of the temple's foundation, made of local volcanic stone, remains behind the original bronze equestrian statue of Marcus Aurelius in the Conservators' Palace.

The larger than life She-Wolf is exhibited on the majestic *piano nobile* (principal floor) of the Palace, where 16th-century frescoes on the 10m-high ceilings depict epic events in the city's history.

In the courtyard are the colossal head and body parts of Constantine *(pictured)*, Rome's first Christian emperor.

The New Wing opposite, which can be reached via an underground passage, contains many inscriptions and Italy's finest collection of busts of emperors, empresses and philosophers, as well as the giant talking statue Marforio (*see p.60*), a reclining river god.

A staircase in the passageway leads up to the 1st-century BC *tabularium* (archives) structure and the adjacent 3rd-century BC Temple of Veiovis, with the 12th-century city hall built over it. Here, through open arches,

PIAZZA DEL CAMPIDOGLIO

The Musei Capitolini occupies two elegant palaces on either side of the Piazza del Campidoglio, which owes its current look to Michelangelo. Commissioned by Pope Paul III Farnese, the versatile Renaissance artist remodelled the space to celebrate a visit by the Holy Roman Emperor Charles V in 1538. His plan included the reworking of the stairs and the piazza to showcase the AD 80 equestrian statue of Marcus Aurelius (a copy now stands in the piazza). Michelangelo also changed the orientation of the government buildings by turning them away from the Classical Forum to face the Vatican.

the panorama of the Roman Forum unfolds.

For an even more splendid panorama, head back to the Conservators' Palace courtyard through to the far right door and entrance to the Palazzo Caffarelli wing. Walk through the Hall of Pediment, with remnants of a 2nd-century terracotta frieze, to the **Caffè Capitolino** (tel: 06-6919 0564; closed Sun), a small coffee bar with an esplanade terrace overlooking both ancient and contemporary Rome. Lunch suggestion: try the *bresaola* – dark cured ham – panino. Entry to the terrace can also be reached from Piazza Caffarelli, the square to the immediate right of the Conservators' Palace.

Capitoline Museums, Piazza del Campidoglio 1; tel: 060608; www.museicapitolini.it; Tue–Sun 9am–8pm; charge; map B4

Slice through an archaeological layer cake at the **church of San Clemente**

The richly decorated Basilica of San Clemente is a typical archaeological layer cake. The Baroque facade hides a 12th-century church built with the columns of a 4th-century church, which in turn sits on a 1st-century *domus* or private house.

The basilica is named after St Clement I, who became a martyr after drowning in the Black Sea in AD 97, and his symbol of anchors can be seen throughout. To reach the original *domus* head two labyrinthine levels underground. On the left on entering is the dining room, converted into a Temple of Mithras in the 2nd century *(pictured)*. A well-preserved altar to the Persian god whose cult spread to Rome is on the far side, and water can be heard from the *horrea*, or warehouse, where an ancient spring still flows.

In the 4th century, a church was built on top of the house. A 6th-century fresco on the right aisle portrays the Madonna as a Byzantine empress. Frescoes record the return of San Clemente's remains to the church in the 9th century, and one features Jesus's harrowing of hell.

Built in 1120, the basilica is embellished with Baroque tombs, early 15th-century frescoes, a 5th-century white marble choir from the church below and a grandiose 12th-century mosaic. Look for the St Catherine chapel with frescoes of the saint painted by Masolino and possibly Masaccio, from around 1425.

After the visit, enjoy Roman cuisine and a jovial family atmosphere at **Le Naumacchie** (Via Celimontana 7; tel: 06-700 2764), just down the street.

Basilica of San Clemente; Via Labicana 95; tel: 06-774 0021; Mon–Sat 9am–12.30pm, 3 –6pm; Sun and public hols noon–6pm; charge; map F3

Be transported back in time to see the **Colosseum** in its full 3-D splendour at **Rome Rewind**

Standing inside the Colosseum on one of its tiers, looking down into the arena, gives a sense of Rome at its most civilised and its most uncivilised. The 50m-high travertine amphitheatre, which could hold 50,000 spectators, is the civilised aspect. But when the Colosseum opened in AD 80, after 10 years of construction under the Emperor Vespasian, the crowd went wild for bloody spectacles. It ran a tight schedule of events from dawn to dusk, including man versus animal fights, noontime executions and afternoon gladiator combat.

Today you can see just how the gladiatorial games were enacted in Rome Rewind, an extraordinary technological achievement that took 30 years to complete. This three-dimensional experience takes you back to the 4th century, through the tunnel of Emperor Commodus to the Colosseum's arena and a roaring crowd. The 3-D movie transports you around a detailed model of ancient Rome, teeming with characters and recognisable major sites of the city.

For a bird's-eye view of the Colosseum, **Aroma** (Via Labicana 125, 06-7759 1380; map F4), the luxurious rooftop restaurant in Palazzo Manfredi, is decidedly romantic, while **Tempio di Iside** (Via Pietro Verri 11; tel: 06-700 4741; map G4) is a small but noteworthy fish restaurant.

Colosseum; Piazza del Colosseo; tel: 06-3996 7700; daily 8.30am–1hr before sunset; charge; map E4
Rome Rewind; Via Capo d'Africa 5; www.3drewind.com; tel: 06-7707 6627; daily 9am–7pm; charge; map E3

Take a break from ancient Rome and the crowds, and **dine in quiet piazza San Teodoro**

Often overlooked, the Velabrum neighbourhood wedged between the Forum and the Capitoline and Palatine hills is a rare quiet corner in the midst of busy Rome. Here, on a raised and seemingly private piazza, is Trattoria San Teodoro, an unusual find in a non-foodie part of town. Their creative interpretation of Roman cuisine and fish dishes makes you want to try everything. Recommended are *piccoli moscardini fritti* (deep-fried baby squid), *triglie, bottarga e carciofi al cartoccio* (red mullet, roe and artichokes baked in a parcel), *alici a beccafico* (pan-fried anchovies with fennel salad), *lasagnetta finissima, scampi, fiori and pecorino* (pasta with scampi, courgette flowers and pecorino cheese) and *sfoglie di mela cotta* (baked apple with cream).

Around the corner is San Teodoro's wine bar and café with a less formal menu and outdoor patio dining.

The nearby Renaissance church **San Giovanni Decollato** has a Giorgio Vasari fresco, *The Beheading of St John*, from 1553.

Trattoria San Teodoro, Via dei Fienili 49–51; tel: 06-678 0933; www.st-teodoro.it; daily lunch and dinner; Nov–Mar closed Sun; map C3

THEATRE OF MARCELLUS

Starting the first week of June and continuing throughout the summer is the evening concert series at the Theatre of Marcellus (Via del Teatro di Marcello 46; tel: 06-8713 1590; www.tempietto.it; map A4–B4) in the Ghetto neighbourhood near San Teodoro. Music programmes range from classic to contemporary. Listening to the music of Liszt, Piazzolla or The Beatles on an inky night under the stars is a cool thing to do on a hot summer night.

Go off-road on **two wheels** (or two feet) on the monument-strewn **Via Appia Antica**

Fresh air is a rare commodity in the city centre, but easy to find in Rome's many parks, especially the Appia Antica Regional Park. Here some sprawling 3,400 hectares of tombs, archaeological sites, Roman villas and catacombs are bisected by the ancient Via Appia, Rome's oldest and longest road. The Appian Way was built in 312 BC and extended 500km to Brindisi on the Adriatic coast. As the last stretch of road home for conquering heroes returning from the east, it became lined with victory monuments and tombs, making it idyllic for a bike or walking tour. Or if you don't want to stretch your legs too much, you can opt for a less energetic tour on the Archeobus.

To cycle, put on your comfortable clothes and head to **Caffè Appia Antica** (Via Appia Antica 175; tel: 338 346 5440; www.appiaanticacaffe.it) where you can rent an inexpensive bike after downing a delicious cappuccino.

For approximately 5km east and west of the café is a non-taxing trail whether by bike or on foot. Heading right out of the café and slightly downhill, you'll find the 1st-century BC Mausoleum of Cecilia Metella and 4th-century AD Villa of Maxentius. On the right and uphill on the left are the catacombs of St Sebastian. Heading east on the modern pavement is the free archaeological site Capo di Bove, an imperial-dated bath complex. At Roman milestone 3, you will encounter the original basalt stone pavement. If you continue to the 5th milestone, you will reach the magnificent 2nd-century AD Villa of the Quintilli, so desired by Emperor Comodus that he killed the brothers Quintilli to take possession of it.

Appia Antica; tel 06-512 6314; www.parcoappiaantica.it; daily 9.30am–4.30pm, until 6.30pm in summer; access via taxi, bus 660 or Archeobus (from Piazza Venezia; tel: 06-684 0901; www.trambusopen.com; map B5)

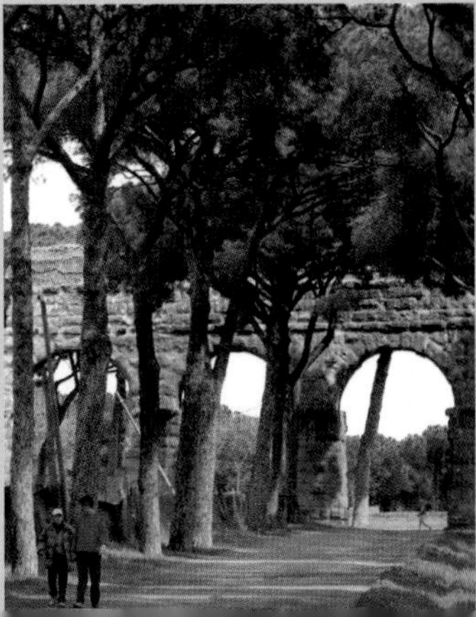

Listen to the wit of Juvenal and the stories of Homer in an **ancient Roman house** at the Case Romane

To the Colosseum's southwest is the Celio, one of Rome's original seven hills and now Villa Celimontana public park. In the midst of the greenery stands the Church of saints John and Paul built on the Case Romane, imperial-era houses. Head to either of the park's two entrances: the monumental gate on Via Celimontana or the picturesque, arched alley of Clivo di Scauro, a sharp incline off the Via San Gregorio facing the Palatine Hill.

On the west side of the church is the entrance to Case Romane, a multi-levelled series of apartments from the 3rd to 12th centuries AD, and a small, very modern museum. The houses, which were at one time transformed into a single luxury house, contained the remains of Paul and John, who were martyred under Emperor Julian in 362, though little else is known of their lives. Thirty years later, a church was built over the house.

The 19th-century finds contain some of Rome's most beautiful frescoes *(pictured)* and mosaic pavements, including a *nymphaeum* (fountain), with a large, detailed mythological fresco, and the Sala dei Genii (Room of the Genii) displaying a frieze of winged male figures holding garlands, surrounded by a multitude of vividly coloured birds.

On select evenings, the Case Romane hosts theatrical performances by actors reciting the works of Juvenal, Homer and others, often accompanied by Roman-inspired antipasti such as *garum* (fermented fish sauce), and an archaeological commentary.

Case Romane del Celio; Clivo di Scauro; tel 06-7045 4544; www.caseromane.it, www.spazioliberocoop.it; Mon, Wed, Fri–Sun 10am–1pm, 3–6pm; charge; map E2

Take a break from sightseeing to **sunbathe** in the afternoon sunshine at the **Circus Maximus**

Circus Maximus is one of the oldest Roman arenas. Not much remains except 70,800 sq m of the vast open space it occupied, making it a good spot to clear your head after a busy morning exploring the ancient sites. It's no surprise that idlers gather here on sunny days. Its slopes are the ideal angle for reading a book while soaking in the afternoon sun or stretching out a picnic blanket for a midday snack. Pick up the goods at **Cristalli di Zucchero** (88; map C3), a pastry shop at the beginning of Via San Teodoro, with a delicious selection of transportable savoury and sweet treats.

Circus Maximus was Rome's largest entertainment stadium, used for chariot racing and animal hunts. Conceived by the Etruscan kings around the 6th century BC as a site for public games, it was expanded in 50 BC by Julius Caesar so that it could hold up to 300,000 spectators. The oval track accommodated 12 chariots and races went for a distance of 6.5km. Today the open fields host special events such as Rome's free New Year's Eve and summer concert series, with stadium blowouts like Genesis, plus other one-off events throughout the year.

Just up the street from Circus Maximus, heading towards the city walls, is the mini-park on Via delle Terme di Caracalla. This is another picturesque Roman setting, but this time designed for more serious physical activity. Wooden workout benches, parallel bars and chin-up bars pepper the open green space, which looks across and into the Baths of Caracalla *(p.159)*.

Circo Massimo; map C2

scarabeo

Trastevere and the Gianicolo

Trastevere and the Gianicolo

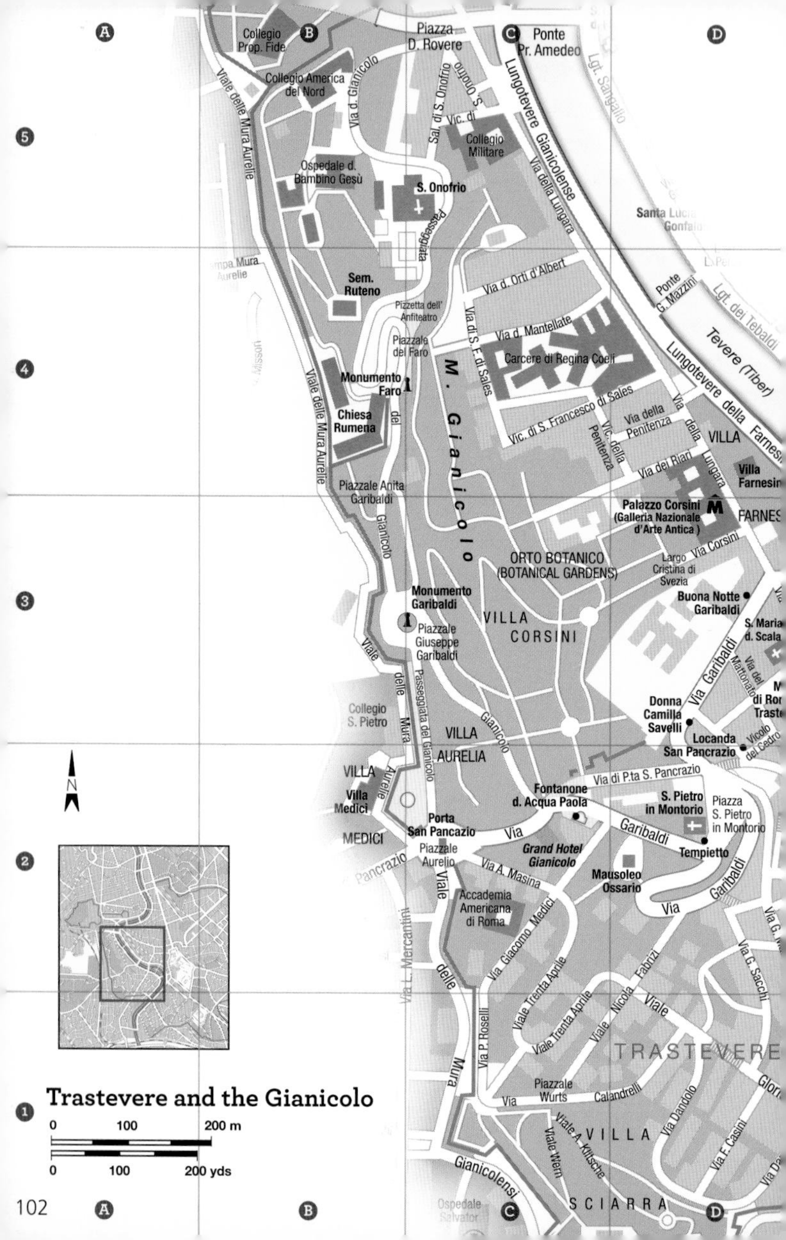

E F G H

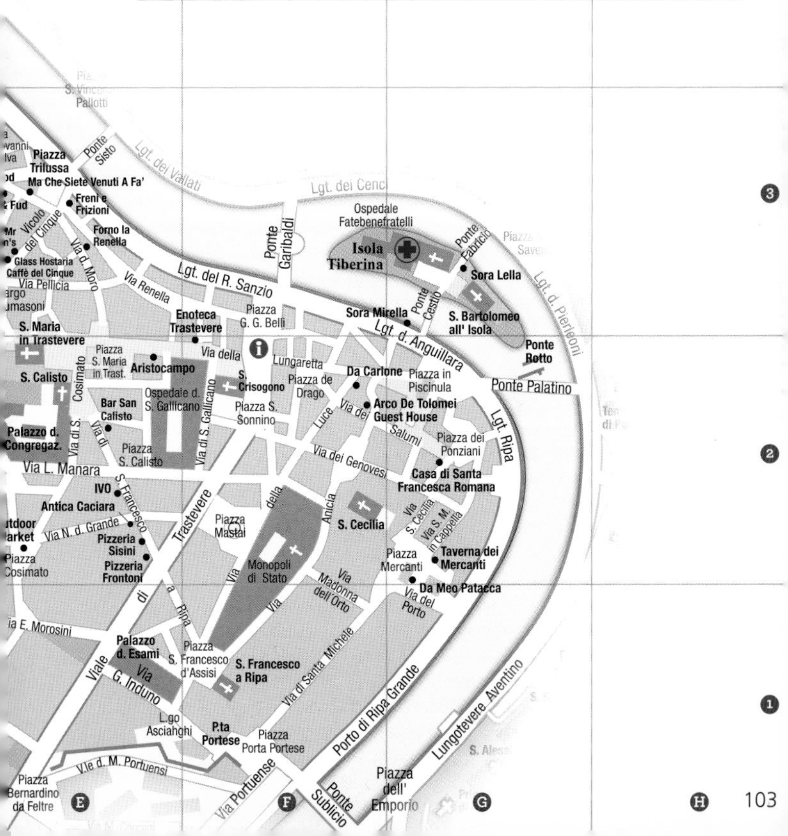

Piazza Trilussa
Ponte Sisto
Lgt. dei Vallati
Lgt. dei Cenci
Ma Che Siete Venuti A Fa'
Freni e Frizioni
Forno la Renella
Vicolo del Cinque
Via d. Moro
Glass Hostaria
Caffè del Cinque
Via Pellicia
Via Renella
Lgt. del R. Sanzio
Ponte Garibaldi
Ospedale Fatebenefratelli
Isola Tiberina
Ponte Fabricio
Sora Lella
Ponte Cestio
Sora Mirella
S. Bartolomeo all' Isola
Lgt. d. Pierleoni
Ponte Rotto
Ponte Palatino
Enoteca Trastevere
Piazza G. G. Belli
S. Maria in Trastevere
Piazza S. Maria in Trast.
Via della Lungaretta
Lgt. d. Anguillara
Da Carlone
Piazza in Piscinula
Aristocampo
S. Calisto
Cosimato
S. Crisogono
Piazza de Drago
Arco De Tolomei Guest House
Ospedale d. S. Gallicano
Via di S. Gallicano
Bar San Calisto
Piazza S. Sonnino
Via dei Salumi
Luce
Piazza dei Ponziani
Lgt. Ripa
Palazzo d. Congregaz.
Via di S.
Via di
Piazza S. Calisto
Via dei Genovesi
Casa di Santa Francesca Romana
Via L. Manara
IVO
S. Francesco
Antica Caciara
Trastevere
della
Anicia
S. Cecilia
Via S. Cecilia
Via S. M. in Cappella
Via N. d. Grande
Pizzeria Sisini
Pizzeria Frontoni
Piazza Mastai
Monopoli di Stato
Piazza Mercanti
Taverna dei Mercanti
Via Madonna dell'Orto
Da Meo Patacca
Via del Porto
Piazza Cosimato
Via E. Morosini
Palazzo d. Esami
Piazza S. Francesco d'Assisi
S. Francesco a Ripa
Via di Santa Michele
Viale
Via G. Induno
Porto di Ripa Grande
Lungotevere Aventino
L.go Asciahghi
P.ta Portese
Piazza Porta Portese
V.le d. M. Portuensi
Via Portuense
Ponte Sublicio
Piazza dell' Emporio
Piazza Bernardino da Feltre

E F G H

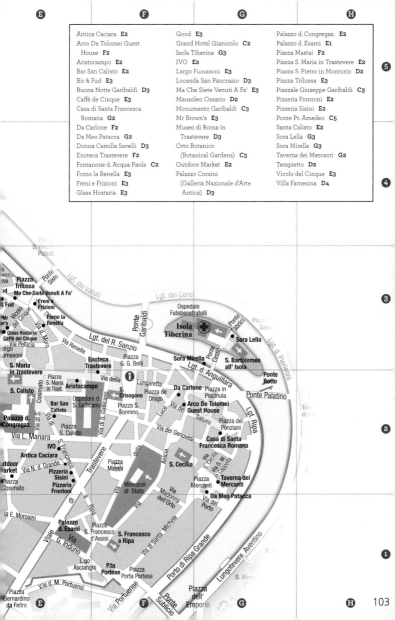

Cool down with **traditional Roman shaved ice** at Sora Mirella

In the hot summer months, those who are still left in the sticky, congested city know that the best way to cool down is with a *grattachecca*, a thirst-quenching concoction of shaved ice, flavoured syrups and fresh fruit. Invented in the 1930s, *grattachecca* ('shave the ice block') kiosks were once a familiar sight on the street corners of Rome. Today, though some kiosks remain, few adopt the traditional hand-grating method.

One of the last authentic *grattachecca* kiosks is Sora Mirella, in front of the Isola Tiberina at Ponte Cestio. Open until late in the evening, the corner is always crowded with customers vying for a Monterosa (strawberry and banana syrups with a squirt of lemon and topped with fresh seasonal fruit) or a Preziosa (made with fresh raspberries, blueberries and strawberries).

The combination of crunchy ice, syrups and fresh fruit is transcendental. While sipping your *grattachecca*, you might forget you are in one of the busiest cities in the world, and instead imagine you are hanging out at a neighbourhood corner with old friends, hypnotised by the animated banter in Roman dialect between the owner's sons and nephews as they grate the ice.

Chiosco della Sora Mirella; Lungotevere degli Anguillara and Ponte Cestio; early spring to autumn daily 9.30am–3am; map G3

Taste Rome's original ***quinto quarto* cuisine** at Ristorante Sora Lella on the **Isola Tiberina**

SUMMER ISLAND

Isola Tiberina is a pretty island that has been associated with healing since a temple to Aesculapius, the Greek god of healing, was built after the city was saved from a plague. There is still a hospital on the island. In summer an outdoor cinema shows current and repertoire films, and multiethnic restaurants collect on its banks. *See www.estateromana.comune.it.*

While nose-to-tail cooking has become *molto* chic in the kitchens of New York and London, the *quinto quarto* has been a working man's staple of *la cucina Romana* for generations. The 'fifth quarter' is what is left of an animal once it has been divided into quarters – in other words offal, all that the working class could afford. To this day there's no Roman *trattoria* worth its salt – or its spleen – that can't whip up a hearty plate of *trippa alla Romana*, tripe slow-cooked in a tomato sauce and finished with *pecorino romano*.

On Isola Tiberina, Sora Lella dishes up a *trippa* with *carciofi alla giudia* (fried artichokes) and other experiences of the *quinto quarto*. Culinary adventurers should try the *taglioni con coratella d'abbachio*, a combination of lamb heart, lungs and liver with *taglioni* pasta, or the comforting *coda alla vaccinara*, braised oxtail. The *frittata alla paesana*, an egg and vegetable baked omelette, will appease lighter stomachs.

Quinto quarto dishes, like tripe, appear on many menus of typical Roman cuisine restaurants, but full immersion in the art of the offal is best experienced here and at **Checchino** and **Da Felice** *(p.162)*.

After dinner, take a walk around the island. In the 2nd century BC the boat shape of the island was accentuated by facing it with travertine and adding nautical ornamentation.

Sora Lella; Via di Ponte Quattro Capi 16; tel: 06-686 1601; www.soralella.it; Mon–Sat 12.30–2.30pm, 8pm–midnight; map G3

Enjoy magical **mosaics of the Virgin Mary** at the church of **Santa Maria in Trastevere**

As the centre of the Roman Catholic world, the city has a special relationship with the Virgin Mary, and no church pays better homage to her than Santa Maria in Trastevere.

The exterior is decorated with a brilliant 12th-century mosaic of the Madonna and Child, surrounded by women holding lamps, the virgins with theirs lit. A visit in the late afternoon is spectacular as the setting sun illuminates the mosaics, creating a heavenly glow.

This is one of Rome's oldest churches. Inside, a series of mosaics and frescoes depict the life and times of Mary. Behind the altar, the restored 13th-century mosaics on the apse ceiling and triumphal arch show the four Evangelists and the prophets Isaiah and Jeremiah. There is also a beautiful interpretation of the *Coronation of the Virgin* in which Christ joins his already crowned mother on the throne.

Beneath these is the work of painter and master restorer Pietro Cavallini. In a nod towards earlier Byzantine mosaic mastery, the artist pieced together a brilliant series of episodes from the Virgin Mary's life. In one scene a flowing stream of olive oil alludes to the legend of the holy site: on the day Christ was born a fountain of oil was said to have erupted on the spot where the church stands.

Before you leave, look for the frescoes to the left of the Baroque Altemps Chapel. A late 16th-century fresco depicts the *Council of Nicea*, and a fresco by Domenichino, of the *Assumption of the Virgin* (1630), graces the ceiling of the nave.

Piazza Santa Maria in Trastevere; tel: 06-581 4802; www.santamariaintrastevere.org; daily 9am–5.30pm; map E2

Kick off a **night on the tiles in Trastevere** at fashionable Freni e Frizioni

Rome's traditional working-class district 'across the Tiber' has always stood apart from the rest of the city. Although it is now the gentrified turf of bourgeois Romans and expats, Trastevere retains a special charm (if you turn a blind eye to the ubiquitous graffiti), especially in the evenings when the bars and restaurants look particularly inviting.

Begin near the Ponte Sisto at the perpetually packed **Freni e Frizioni**, 'Breaks and Clutches', in an old mechanic's shop (Via Politeama 4–6; map E3). Like most of Trastevere's bars, Freni's casual cool is best enjoyed outside among the hordes of the hip. Come between 7pm and 10pm for the *aperitivo*, snacks and salads.

Finish your sundowner and descend the steps into Piazza Trilussa (map E3), the neighbourhood's heart. Stop by **Enoteca Ferrara** (41) for a sophisticated *vino* or Prosecco, or cross the piazza for artisanal beers and paprika and liquorice potato chips at **Bir & Fud** (Via Benedetta 23; map E3). Across the street at 25 is **Ma Che Siete Venuti A Fa'** (slang for 'What the hell are you doing here?'), also known as 'The Football Pub' for its banners and love of the sport, serving beers from around Europe.

More raucous haunts line Vicolo del Cinque (map E3). **Mr Brown's** (29) serves strong, cheap cocktails, or wander a little further up the street to the popular **Caffè del Cinque** (5). Continue the revelry at **Artù** (Largo Fumasoni Biondi 5; map E3), nestled in a gorgeous medieval building. The service can be maddening, but there's no better spot to allow the city's grand history to seep in.

Late at night, every Roman eventually finds him or herself at **Bar San Calisto** (Piazza San Calisto 5; map E2), a timeless classic on the other side of Piazza Santa Maria. The atmosphere is authentic, but it can be claustrophobic – standing outside is the only option.

Absorb an **iconic view of the city** from Rome's largest fountain, the **Fontanone**

The monumental Fountain of Acqua Paola occupies a prime position on top of the Gianicolo hill overlooking the whole of Rome. This sweeping vista spans the rooftops from the Olympic Stadium in the north to the buildings of EUR in the south, making this the perfect look-out point and photo opportunity.

Commissioned by Pope Paul V in 1612, the fountain was built from a ruined aqueduct as a source of drinking water for residents on the Gianicolo hill. Though officially named after the pope, this majestic fountain – the emblem of the Gianicolo neighbourhood – is more commonly and fondly referred to as the Fontanone, 'the big fountain'. Its five arches are reminiscent of ancient triumphal arches, and it is made from marble taken from the 1st-century Temple of Minerva in the Forum of Nerva on the Via dei Fori Imperiali. Water cascades from the three central niches into a large, semicircular basin.

In summer, the garden terrace of the Fontanone provides a cool escape from the city heat and becomes the backdrop to **Fontanone Estate**, an outdoor evening bar and café with music and DJ (www.estateromana.comune.it). The green space across the Via Giacomo Medici, is used to stage open-air cinema evenings, screening classics and arthouse film favourites.

Daytime visitors should walk to the centre of the park and around the Fascist-era mausoleum. The **Ossario Mausoleum** (Via Garibaldi 29a; Tue–Sun 9am–1pm) commemorates the soldiers in Garibaldi's army who fell defending Rome against the French in 1849, and the rebels executed in the insurrections of 1868 and 1870.

Fontanone (Fontana dell'Acqua Paola); Via Garibaldi 53; map C2

Brush up on **High Renaissance style** at Bramante's tiny **Tempietto**

Considered one of the most harmonious monuments in Rome, the Tempietto is a hidden jewel on the Gianicolo's crest. On the grounds of the Spanish Embassy and next to the Church of San Pietro in Montorio is the courtyard sheltering Donato Bramante's 'little temple'. Whether peeking through the gate or walking around the courtyard, you cannot help but be entranced by this small chapel that marks the traditional location of St Peter's crucifixion.

Built in 1502, at the height of the Renaissance, the round chapel is a nod both to the beauty of classical antiquity and to Filippo Brunelleschi, architect of the famous duomo in Florence. The design of the two-storey white marble building is simple and devoid of unnecessary detail. The first level is encircled by 16 granite columns, while the second storey is surrounded by a circular balustrade. The upper part was originally just a hemispherical dome, and a crowning ornament was later placed on top of it.

In contrast, the interior is highly decorated with frescoes and sculptural relief from Renaissance and Baroque artists, including man-about-town Gianlorenzo Bernini. Step back into the piazza below for another view of the Tempietto. Raised on a platform, the small temple looks as if it wants to burst upward and out of the small courtyard.

A walk around the piazza reveals other secrets. On the side of the church in Via Garibaldi, a cannonball is stuck to the brick wall to remind Romans of the 1849 battle for the city.

Back in the piazza you will see an ivy-covered gate opposite. When open, you'll find a romantic short cut to Trastevere.

Tempietto; Piazza San Pietro in Montorio; tel: 06-581 3940; www.sanpietroinmontorio.it; Tue–Sat 9.30am–12.30pm, 2–4.30pm; free; map D2

Grab a bite to go with ***supplì al telefono, pizza al taglio*** and other tasty **Trastevere street food**

The best way to get to know Trastevere is by walking its timeless streets with a bit of local flavour in your hand. Whether you're trying to cram in one last afternoon tour or you're just hungry, indulge your senses with the sights, smells and tastes of *la cucina per strada* (street food).

Pizza al taglio (by the slice) is the unquestioned king of Roman street food, and there is no better neighbourhood than Trastevere for an aimless stroll with this savoury treat. Unlike the round version from the *pizzeria*, these are baked in long rectangular pans with almost no limit to the toppings and combinations, and are cut to the size you want.

Just off busy Piazza Trilussa, **Forno la Renella** (Via del Moro 15; map E3) is a traditional bakery serving pizza and *focaccia* the way they're meant to be. Churning out a flaky, thick crust, Forno la Renella showcases the artisanal tradition of the neighbourhood's past. South of Piazza Santa Maria in Trastevere, **Pizzeria Sisini** (Via di San Francesco a Ripa; map E2) is where the *cognoscenti* go to battle for some of the finest *pizza al taglio* in the city.

If you feel a bit pizza-ed out, go for *suppli al telefono* (deep-

fried rice balls unique to Rome). When cooked properly, the sturdy exterior of the *suppli* should give way to a cushion of risotto cooked in a light tomato sauce. After one or two bites, you'll discover the true reward – a lovely ball of *mozzarella di bufala* waiting in the centre. When you bite into it, the cheese should string out like a telephone cord, hence *al telefono*.

Pizzeria Frontoni (Viale di Trastevere 52; map E2), and round-the-corner rival **Ivo** (Via di San Franscesco a Ripa 158; map E2), battle for title of best *suppli al telefono*, although **Franchi** *(p.80)* has long held the title of best *suppli* in the entire city.

For something more substantial, visit one of the neighbourhood's panino shops serving *porchetta*, slices of spiced roasted pig from the Castelli Romani hills just outside the city. Traditionalists go for the *panino rustica* – slices of this delectable pork on a plain roll – but at **Aristocampo** (Via della Lungaretta 75; map E2) you can experiment with combinations. Try adding spinach and *scamorza* (smoked cheese) or even sauerkraut and mustard.

Another simple delight is the *tramezzino*, found in almost every neighbourhood café. These delicate sandwiches can be lightly toasted and filled with such combos as tuna and artichoke, spinach and mozzarella, or egg, tomato and mayo. They are made of crust-less white bread in triangular shapes – just like mamma made. Be careful of a day-old trammy: too-yellow mayo, wilted lettuce or hardening bread. But the pleasure of ordering *prosciutto e formaggio, un po' scaldato* (warmed up), and getting a grilled cheese and ham sandwich, is usually worth the risk. Perfect for picky kids.

Walk among **exotic and rare plants** in **Botanical Gardens** that once belonged to the pope

Rolling over 12 hectares of the Gianicolo hill slopes towards Trastevere are Rome's Botanical Gardens. More than 3,000 species of plants and trees grow here. Founded in the 13th century for the Vatican, it was officially given to the Gianicolo in 1660 as part of the University of Rome.

You'll delight in becoming lost among its bamboo groves, rose beds, fern paths, Japanese garden, and the tranquil rock garden. But eventually you will find your way to two particular enclosures: the Giardini degli Aromi, a star-shaped, scented garden, and the Orto dei Semplici, a medicinal herb garden. A plethora of herbs, we are told, cause moderate to severe digestive reactions, perhaps harking back to the days when Pope Alexander VI strolled the grounds. He was the father of Lucrezia Borgia whose three marriages all ended in the not-so-natural deaths of her husbands.

A path winds around rococo fountains, a pond with aquatic flowers, an untouched ancient woodland and a grove of pine trees from all over the world.

The botanical garden is the backyard of the **Palazzo Corsini** where the path ends. The former patrician palace is the National Gallery of Antique Art, with a collection of paintings from the early Renaissance to the late 18th century. Here Caravaggio fans will find *St John the Baptist*, one of Rome's 29 paintings by the 17th-century artist *(p.34)*. Compare it to a painting of the same subject by his friend Guido Reni, which is also in the collection.

Orto Botanico; Largo Cristina di Svezia 24; tel: 06-686 4193; Mon–Sat 9am–7pm, until 6pm in winter; charge; map C3
Palazzo Corsini; Via della Lungara 10; tel: 06-6880 2323; Tue–Sun 9am–2pm; www.galleriaborghese.it; charge; map D3

Entertain your kids with parks, puppets and ponies on the **Piazzale Giuseppe Garibaldi**

The Gianicolo, the highest hill within ancient Rome's walls, has a wonderful view of the city and offers respite for worn-out children and their parents. Head to the top at Piazzale Garibaldi, named after revolutionary Giuseppe Garibaldi whose equestrian statue marks the square's centre. In 1849, Garibaldi lost the battle with the Roman Republic and papal-backed French troops, but it proved only a temporary setback for the hero of Italian unification.

From Piazza Garibaldi's terrace, Rome's rooftops, domes and towers are always in dazzling array. Take the road to the right, Passeggiata del Gianicolo, to the *parco dei giochi*, a children's park with a roundabout and pony rides.

On the north extension of Passeggiata del Gianocolo, amid food and refreshment stands, is the **Teatro dei Burratini di Carlo Piantandosi**, Rome's historic puppet theatre. The Piantandosi have been amusing children for decades with performances throughout the day. The handmade wooden puppets represent classic characters from the 16th-century Commedia dell'Arte – Pulcinella, Arlecchino, Colombina and Pantalone.

Make sure to cover your ears at 11.59am. At noon on the dot, a historic cannon is fired beneath the piazza's plateau, a tradition started by Pope Pius IX to synchronise the bells of Rome.

Piazzale Garibaldi; map C3

Step into a Renaissance love nest decorated by Raphael at the **Villa Farnesina**

In 1518, the artist Raphael Sanzio was rumoured to have locked himself away in the Villa Farnesina, the suburban Renaissance villa of a banker, Agostino Chigi, in order to get over a broken heart. Whether true or not, heartaches and secret trysts were the main commodity at the villa. Villa Farnesina was built as a weekend getaway for Chigi to play host to his favourite courtesans, in particular Imperia, who was then the most famous in the city.

To depict erotic mythological scenes throughout the villa, Chigi hired a bevy of painters including Raphael, Baldassare Peruzzi and Sebastiano del Piombo. The ground-floor *Loggia of Galatea,* from around 1512, depicts scenes from Ovid's *Metamorphosis* and and has Chigi's zodiacal signs on its ceiling. Raphael's lustrous *Triumph of Galatea* appears on the main wall, riding a shell-shaped chariot, reminiscent of Botticelli's *Birth of Venus*, while the surrounding nymphs and sea creatures recall Michelangelo's contorting figures in the Sistine Chapel. Some believe that Galatea is a portrait of Imperia, who poisoned herself after hearing that Chigi was to marry another woman. But most art historians believe Galatea is Raphael's interpretation of Ideal Beauty.

In 1518, Raphael returned to the villa to paint the *Loggia of Cupid and Psyche* with ceiling frescoes telling the legend of Cupid and Psyche, pictured here. Again, Imperia is said to have been the inspiration for Psyche, goddess of the soul, who, after a convoluted tale of jealousies and gods, marries Cupid.

Villa Farnesina, Via della Lungara 230; www.villafarnesina.it; tel 06-6802 7267; Mon–Sat 9am–1pm; charge; map D4

Step back in time to **medieval Trastevere** in **Piazza de' Mercanti**

Trastevere is often billed as the only 'real' Roman neighbourhood. True Trasteverini families, often working-class, have lived here for centuries, and the proud few who remain represent the highest concentration of Romanesco speakers – a dialect of sliced syllables and Latin words.

In the late 1970s and '80s, the neighbourhood began to gentrify. As a result, a true local experience here is hard to find. But in the impossibly charming Piazza de' Mercanti on the southern, less trafficky side of the neighbourhood, the clock is turned back.

At night, the piazza, fringed with ivy-covered buildings, is illuminated by torch light and glowing cobblestones. At **Taverna dei Mercanti** (3; tel: 06-588 1693), an ancient torchlit building decked with flowers, excellent thin-crust Roman pizza is served. Take a peek at the 16th-century ceiling inside: the taverna was an inn for weary riders and their horses.

Around the corner, Remington Olmstead, an American actor from the 1930s silver screen, has captured an ersatz Trastevere. **Da Meo Patacca** (30; tel: 06-581 6198; dinner only) is an adventure in vintage Trastevere with a typical Roman menu and kitschy costumed waiters who act like Meo Patacca, a lazy and quarrelsome tough guy from the *Commedia dell'Arte*.

Piazza de' Mercanti; map G2

MUSEUM OF ROME

For a fascinating insight into Roman life in the 18th and 19th centuries, visit the Museo di Roma (Piazza Sant'Egidio; tel: 06-581 6563; www.museodiromaintrastevere.it; Tue–Sun 10am–8pm; charge; map E3) in central Trastevere. The small museum, housed in a beautifully restored Carmelite convent, has a collection of costumes, art and crafts. One corner of the museum is occupied by **Le Scene Romane**, life-sized dioramas of scenes from 18th-century life, from a visit to the pharmacy to dancing at an inn.

Discover a hidden Roman house and the story of a martyred saint at the **Basilica of Saint Cecilia**

A question to ask yourself when in Rome is 'What's underneath?' Almost every building hides fragments of the past. The Basilica di Santa Cecilia, above the house of the martyred saint in the southernmost part of Trastevere, provides an excellent opportunity to investigate this question.

The entrance to the 3rd-century house is via the sacristy on the left aisle of the 9th-century church. Head downstairs to walk through the ruins of a house with mosaic pavements, early Christian sarcophagi and a small museum with a household shrine to the goddess Minerva.

Saint Cecilia, the patron saint of music, was thought to have been a noblewoman who owned the central *domus* in a neighbourhood that included a tannery and bathhouse. In AD 230, after she and her husband converted to Christianity, she was sentenced to death by scalding in her own bathhouse. When this failed, she was to be beheaded, but three strokes of the axe failed to despatch her and she lived for three days before dying.

Upstairs is Stefano Maderno's 17th-century sculpture of the saint with the axe marks on her neck. In the apse is a 9th-century mosaic, and in the Chapel of the Bath a canvas of the saint's coronation by Guido Reni.

Before leaving the charming 13th-century courtyard, look to the immediate left of the entrance to see the imperial boundary stone of ancient Rome.

Saint Cecilia in Trastevere; Piazza Santa Cecilia 22; tel: 06-589 9289; daily 10am–noon, 4–6pm; charge; map F2

Try the (debatably) best **real carbonara** at Remo and Bettina's Da Carlone

A dish that dates back 150 years and is named after the charcoal burners who cooked it over the *carbone* (charcoal), spaghetti *alla carbonara* is an essential experience for any visitor. As with all things Roman, this dish is the subject of a much-heated debate as to whose creation reigns supreme.

On a quiet, narrow Trastevere street near the Isola Tiburina, Da Carlone has been dishing up the best plate (arguably, of course) of this quintessential Roman pasta since the early 1900s. The preparation is deceptively simple: sautéed *guanciale* (bite-size bits of pig cheek), eggs, pasta and liberal amounts of grated Pecorino Romano and freshly ground black pepper. The pasta is dipped into the egg yolk at the last minute then tossed with the meat, cheese and pepper.

Remo, the Abruzzese owner, likes to amble out onto the street in his yolk-stained apron to survey the delight on his patrons' faces as they devour plate after plate of this magical dish, though it is his wife, Bettina, who stays behind the scenes to churn out such generous heaps of perfection. And just in case you're not convinced of the supremacy of their effort, take notice of the old charcoal storage depot right across the street. You can just imagine the old charcoal burners cooking up their lunch, and passing on their recipe to Remo's ancestors.

Other great restaurants (and more arguments) for authentic pasta include **Il Matriciano** *(p.71)* and **Colline Emiliane** *(p.61)*, both family-run.

Antica Trattoria Da Carlone; Via della Luce 5; tel: 06-580 0039; Tue–Sun 12.30–2.30pm, 7.30–11pm; map F2

Pack your **picnic basket** at the century-old **Antica Caciara *gastronomia***

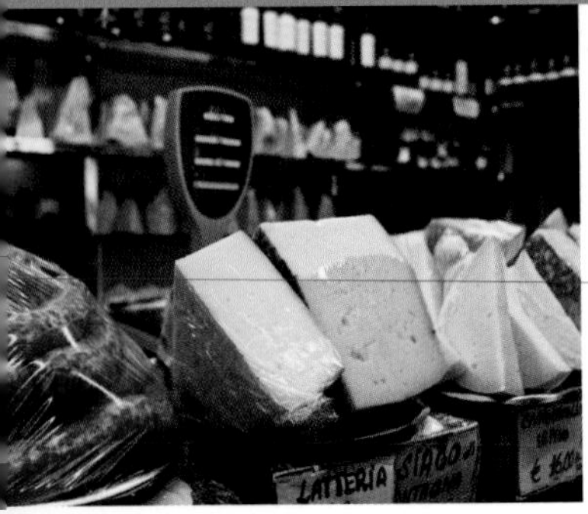

In the wee hours of the morning, local shepherds deliver fresh ricotta to Antica Caciara, a timeless neighbourhood *gastronomia* (delicatessen), and by mid-morning it has disappeared. Rows of wines and oils, prosciutto, salami and cured meats on hooks, a counter packed with mozzarella, burrata (cheese made from mozzarella and cream), pesto and baccalà (salt cod) – it's the right place for picnic packing.

The ever polite Roberto patiently lets you sample his wares, including his favourites: *lardo di Colonnata*, the Tuscany pork delicacy, *ubriacone al teroldego*, creamy sheep's milk cheese brined in Teroldego wine, and of course *pecorino Romano*, local sheep's milk cheese. His cheeses have a personal touch. *Pecorino di fossa*, also from sheep's milk, is wrapped in cloth and placed in a subterranean cave on a bed of burnt straw covered with sand and pebbles and left to mature for 100 days.

At the end of a sale, Roberto shakes your hand, a forgotten etiquette much appreciated. Now head up to the Gianicolo for a picnic with a view of Rome, or to Piazza San Cosimato *(see below)* behind Antica Caciara for a glimpse of daily Trastevere life.

Antica Caciara Trasteverina; Via di San Francesco a Ripa 140 a/b; tel: 06-581 215; www.anticacaciara.it; Mon–Sat 7am–2pm, 4–8pm; map E2

PIAZZA SAN COSIMATO MARKET

Just up the hill from Antica Caciara Trastevere is Piazza San Cosimato (map E2) where every morning (except on Sundays) local vendors sell fresh produce, meats, fish and flowers in a recently modernised market. The corner flower shop along Via di San Cosimato claims papal envoys come to pick out weekly arrangements. On the opposite side of the market, in Via Roma Libera, is the neighbourhood rock star cheese vendor Emiliano (and parents), whose salami-draped guitar-in-hand photo hangs on the wall. Cheese selection reaches far beyond Italy and includes the fine French *mimolette*.

Savour a **glass of wine and catch up on your emails** in a comforting *enoteca*

If you need to send any emails in Rome, and haven't mastered the trying task of hotel Wi-fi, head for **Good Caffè**, which has what must be the most pleasant internet experience in Italy. A rustic wine bar on the ground floor in an ivy-covered medieval palazzo, Good wins as the most picturesque Wi-fi spot. In contrast to the stark decor of the average internet café, this is a cosy, traditional *enoteca*, with wine bottles lining the dark wooden walls, and tables indoor and out that accommodate your glass of Barolo and laptop. You must have your own device, whether laptop or smart phone. Wi-fi shuts down by 6.30pm, when a DJ begins to prepare for the 7.30pm *aperitivi* set.

If you don't have a laptop to hand but still fancy a delicious glass of wine away from the clamour of Trastevere central, yet deep in the heart of this medieval neighbourhood, visit **Enoteca Trastevere**. This traditional wine bar has all the right trappings – beamed wooden ceilings, candlelight, hushed voices and satisfying antipasti. The *enoteca* draws in the neighbourhood crowd who want to enjoy a glass of wine, *sans* internet and chaos. For the novice sommelier, have fun tasting rare vintages from the extensive wine selection. And gastronomes, prepare yourselves for their specialities: *prosciutto di cervo o cinghiale* (wild boar or deer prosciutto), polenta with porcini mushrooms, and *zuppa di farro e legumi* (soup made with barley and vegetables).

Good Caffè, Via di Santa Dorotea 89; tel: 06-9727 7979; Mon–Sat 7am–2am; map E3
Enoteca Trastevere; Via della Lungaretta 86; tel: 06-588 5659; Thur–Tue lunch and dinner; map F2

Villa Borghese, Via Veneto and Flaminia

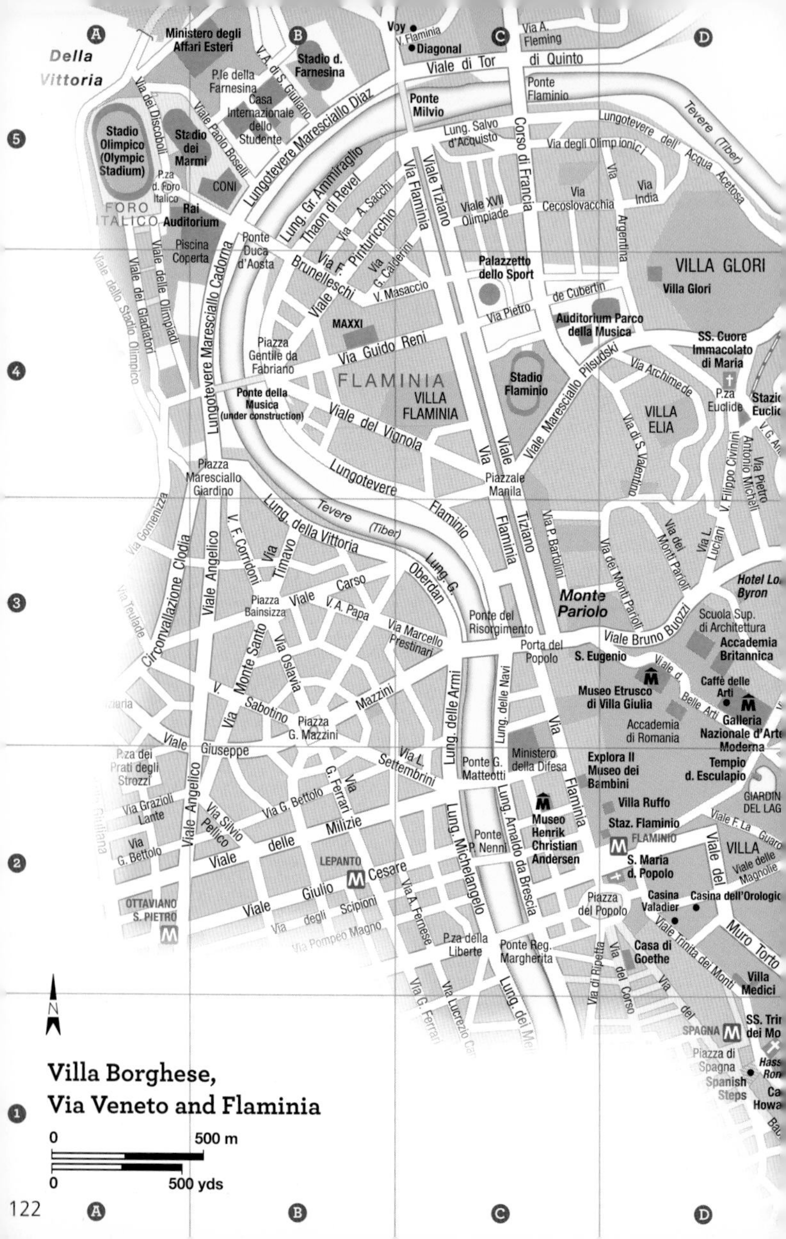

Villa Borghese, Via Veneto and Flaminia

E
F
G
H
5
4
3
2
1
PARIOLI
Via Ruggero Fauro
Via G. Castellini
Via Antonio
Via F. Siacci
Bruno Buozzi
PINCIANO
P.za Ungheria
Viale
V.G. Rossini
Via G. Pinciana
V.G. d'Arezzo
Istituto
dello Stato
Museo Africano
Museo Civico di Zoologia (Zoo)
Bioparco
V. Mercadante
Giardino Zoologico
Grand Hotel Parco dei Principi
PARCO DEI PRINCIPI
V.P. Raimondi
Via J. Peri
Via Salaria
Via Po
Museo Canonica
V.le dell' Uccelliera
Galleria Borghese
Mausoleo d. Lucillo Petro
V.le dei Cavalli Marini
Piazza di Siena
SALARIO
BORGHESE
Casina di Raffaello
Via Isonzo
S. Teresa
P.za Fiume
V.le Goethe
V.le del Museo Borghese
Via Pinciana
Corso d'Italia
P.le Brasile
Chiesa Luterana
Via Piave
Porta Pinciana
Via Sicilia
S. Patrizio
Gargani
Il Chicco
Via Veneto
Hotel Eden
Via Ludovisi
Palazzo Margherita
Via Sallustiana
Via G. Carducci
V. Liguria
Via Leonida Bissolati
Piazza Barberini
Sistina
Via del Tritone
Palazzo Barberini
Via XX Settembre
GIARDINO DEL QUIRINALE
E
F
G
H

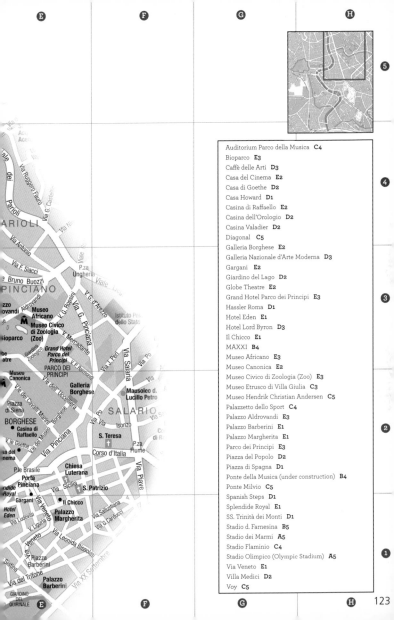

Ride a bike, row a boat and discover your inner child in the **Villa Borghese park**

Rome's best-loved park is the heart-shaped Villa Borghese gardens, on the Pincio hill above Piazza del Popolo. Unfolding over 60 hectares, it is the place to escape to when you need to unleash your child – or your inner child.

The gardens were developed for the villa of Cardinal Scipione Borghese, nephew of Pope Paul V, in 1605, and landscaped in the English style in the 19th century. Casts of statues pepper the park – the originals are in New York's Metropolitan Museum of Art.

At the Viale San Paolo del Brasile entrance (near Via Veneto) park yourself at the outdoor café of the **Casa del Cinema** (tel: 06-423 601; E2). A great place for liquid refreshments, you can hone your film knowledge at the bookstore, catch a classic or soon-to-be-classic film in its indoor screening rooms (mostly in Italian) and in summer enjoy films under the night sky.

Across the green is an old-fashioned roundabout, quadri-cycle and bicycle rentals (there are pick-up-and-drop stations throughout the park), and the **Cinema dei Piccoli**, a 63-seat cinema for children. The electric St Peter's train – for adults and children – runs from nearby Viale Goethe across to Galleria Borghese *(p.126)*. To its immediate north is the **Bioparco di Roma** (map E3), a zoo and conservation centre. One of its most popular residents is a young hippopotamus named Pipa.

Roaming the central area of the park, you'll find a reconstruction of the **Globe Theatre** (map E2), with summer evening performances of Shakespeare (in Italian), the **Piazza di Siena** (map E2) race track, which hosts international equestrian events at the end of May, and the **Casina di Raffaello** (map E3), an indoor/outdoor children's area with educational programmes.

In the heart of the park is the **Giardino del Lago** (map D2), with a picturesque lake, floating island temple and rowing boats for hire.

The Viale delle Magnolie, lined with monumental magnolia trees, lies in the western area and leads to the turn-of-the-century **Casina**

THE GARDENS OF LUCULLUS

Villa Borghese Gardens are on the site of the Gardens of Lucullus, a feature of 1st-century BC Rome. Lucullus had military triumphs in the East, bringing back huge amounts of booty, and the inspiration, from the Persians, to start his gardens here. He is credited with introducing sweet cherry and apricot trees to the West.

dell'Orologio (tel: 06-679 8515; map D2), an old-fashioned café and clock tower with delicious lunch menu and home-made *gelato*.

The surrounding area is where kids of all sizes have fun with bike, rollerblade and skate rentals.

Teatro Marionette San Carlino (Sat and Sun only) is an opera house miniature for puppet shows. Sometimes, fresh candy- floss is sold here.

Villa Borghese Park; map D2-3, E2-3

Gianlorenzo Bernini is uncontestedly Rome's most prolific artist. Brilliantly touching nearly every palace and square in the city, his sublime sculpture and virtuoso architectural design gave Roman Baroque its theatrical flair.

To see the very best of his sculpture, visit the two-storey Galleria Borghese, an early 17th-century mini-villa and art gallery in Villa Borghese. Four Bernini masterpieces take centre stage, though Canova is also here, with Pauline Bonaparte as *Venus Victrix* *(p.43)* in the entrance hall.

Room II has Bernini's 1623 *David*, and Room III a lively sculpture of *Apollo and Daphne* (1622–5).

Room IV, known as the Gallery of the Emperors for its collection of imposing imperial busts, has Bernini's dynamic *Rape of Proserpine* (1621–2; *pictured*). Hades' hand grips Proserpine's left thigh, and in the afternoon light you can feel his fingers digging into her peerless marble flesh.

Head through to Room VI, the Room of the Gladiator, where *Aeneas, Anchises and Ascanius*, (1618–9) depicts the flight from Troy. The two small figures in Anchises' hands are Romulus and Remus. In the corner is Bernini's unfinished *Truth* (1642).

Room VIII, Gallery of Silenus, has six Caravaggio paintings including two self-portraits – *Il Bacchino Malato* (1593) and *David with Head of Goliath* (1609–10).

Back in the Gallery of the Emperors, stairs lead to the grandiose Gallery of Lanfranco. where you can compare Bernini's self-portraits, from 1623 and 1635.

Galleria Borghese; Piazzale del Museo Borghese 5; tel: 06-32810; www.galleriaborghese.it; Tue–Sun 8.30am–7.30pm; charge; map E2

Have a **gourmet feast** while watching the sun bathe the Eternal City at the **Casina Valadier**

Casina Valadier is a neoclassical trophy perched on the edge of the Pincio hill. It was designed in the early 19th century by Giuseppe Valadier as a meeting place, in a French bistro style. Restored in 2004, the Casina reopened as a luxury gourmet restaurant. On the edge of Villa Borghese with a classic view of Rome and Vatican City, it is a romantic sunset spot.

The colonnaded terrace's lavish Pompeiian-style ceiling continues throughout the Casina, but the glass-enclosed dining room with a never-ending panorama is where you want to be.

The menu offers imaginative interpretations of regional Italian cuisine such as *maltagliati farciti con ricotta in salsa di pachino* (home-made, 'badly cut' pasta pieces with ricotta cheese in a tomato sauce), duck breast *carpaccio*, and fried courgette flowers stuffed with rice and served with cinnamon ice cream.

Take a peek at the Sala Romana wine cellar. It was found during the restoration when a cistern was uncovered under the foundation.

Other perspectives from the Pincio can be found in beautiful, smart hotel restaurants (no jeans or shorts) with views, such as Michelin-starred **Mirabelle** on the 7th floor of the Baroque 5-star Splendide Royal (Via di Porta Pinciana 14; tel: 06-4216 8838; map E1); the 6th-floor **Imàgo** at the Hassler hotel (Piazza Trinità dei Monti 6; tel: 06-699 340; D1), where the maître d' will point out the sights as well as the dishes of regional cuisine; and **La Terrazza** at Hotel Eden (Via Ludovisi 49; tel: 06-478 121; map E1), where Mediterranean dishes have a piano accompaniment.

Casina Valadier; Piazza Bucarest; tel: 06-6992 2090 (reservations required); www.casinavaladier.it; Tue–Sat 12.30–3pm, 8–11pm, Sun 12.30–3pm; map D2

Show your true colours at a **football derby** at the **Olympic Stadium**

RUGBY AND ROME
Both Roma and Lazio initiated rugby union teams in the late 1920s, and though they didn't survive, Rugby Roma Olimpic, which today plays in the top Super 10 league, came out of their demise in 1930. More popular in northern Italy, the game took off in 2000 when the Italians turned Europe's Five Nations League into the Six Nations League, with Rome's **Stadio Flaminio** serving as home to the national team, the Azzuri (the blues). Roma Olimpic plays at the Tre Fontane Stadium, and if you can score tickets for either stadium, the atmosphere is jovial with plenty of good-natured banter between fans.

'Sei Laziale o Romanista?' Are you a Lazio or a Roma fan? This is the most important question you will be asked when in Rome. The rivalry between the two home teams runs deep and your answer can open or close doors. Twice a year, you will need to take a distinct stand as the Olympic Stadium, Rome's football pitch, hosts the derby, in what is the most intense atmosphere since the days of the gladiators.

A visit to the stadium, whether on a game day or not, is always interesting. A 10-minute tram ride from the city centre, the stadium was constructed in 1931 under Benito Mussolini as part of the Foro Italico sports complex. Traces of the Fascist dictator are everywhere: a 17.5m white marble obelisk inscribed *DUX* (latin for *Il Duce* or leader, which is what Mussolini liked to be called) greets you as you walk across a mosaic pavement that records Roman accomplishments.

To the Olimpico's immediate east is the Stadio dei Marmi, a marble stadium with 60 idealised athletic figures, reminiscent of Ancient Rome.

Stadio Olimpico; Via Foro Italico; www.asroma.it, www.sslazio.it; Metro A to Flaminio, then tram 2 to Piazza Mancini; map A5

Sip **cocktails poolside** and savour delicious *tramezzini* at the **Parco dei Principi Hotel**

Poolside cocktails are never a maybe when the bathing spot is a fabulous F. Scott Fitzgerald kind of place. In the backyard of the 5-star Parco dei Principi Hotel, designed in the 1960s by Gio Ponti, is a luxurious Olympic-sized outdoor pool. From the setting - the hotel's botanical garden, among pines and ancient ruins - to the fabulous furniture design - minimal 1960s-style deckchairs and couches - the atmosphere is very *Tender is the Night*. Poolside attendants are alert to your needs, and the quaint pool bar serves delectable *tramezzini* and other savoury snacks with any cocktail you care to invent.

On the hill above the Colosseum, **All'Ombra del Colosseo** (Via di San Gregorio; www.allombradelcolosseo.it) sets up a summer country club with a temporary pool and cabana boys. Other lovely outdoor pools include the rooftop bathing hotels at the **Radisson** (Via Filippo Turati, 171; www.radissonblu.com/eshotel-rome) by the station and Piazza Repubblica's **Hotel Exedra** (Piazza della Repubblica, 47; *see p.172*), and garden pools at **Grand Hotel del Gianicolo** (Viale delle Mura Gianicolensi 107; map p.102 C2), **Aldrovandi Palace** (Via Ulisse Aldrovandi, 15; map E3) and **Cavalieri Hilton** *(see p.173)*.

Parco dei Principi Hotel; Via Gerolamo Frescobaldi 5; tel: 06-854 421; www.parcodeiprincipi.com; map E3

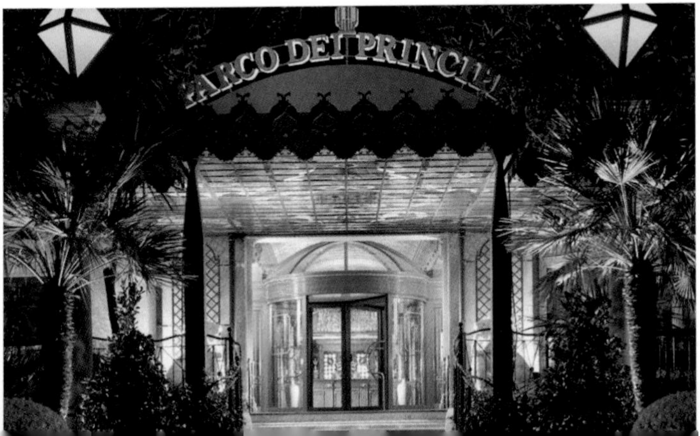

Muse over modern masterpieces and then enjoy a lazy lunch at the **National Gallery of Modern Art**

After spending days knee-deep in classical history, a touch of Marinetti and his fellow Futuristi will help to bring you up to date. On the north edge of Villa Borghese is the neoclassical National Gallery of Modern and Contemporary Art, a 75-room museum containing the most comprehensive collection of 19th- and 20th-century Italian art.

Dominating the rooms are the Italian Futurists, a social and artistic movement from 1909–1916 celebrating technology and industry, championed by artists Giacomo Balla, Umberto Boccioni and F.T. Marinetti. You'll also encounter paintings and sculptures by well-known 20th-century Italian artists such as Modigliani, Giorgio Morandi, Giorgio di Chirico, Pietro Manzoni and Francesco Clemente. Plus, the museum has a small but strong collection of work by Edgar Degas, Marcel Duchamp, Jackson Pollock, Yves Klein, Wassily Kandinsky, Cy Twombly and Sol LeWitt.

Hidden behind the Corinthian columns, on the Gallery's west side, the **Caffè delle Arti** (tel: 06-3265 1236) is a good spot for lunch or an *aperitivo*. For a more languorous lunch, there is a formal restaurant, but those in the know head to the bar for a cappuccino or *shakerato* (iced coffee) at the counter or at an outdoor table with waiter service.

Galleria Nazionale d'Arte Moderna; Viale delle Belle Arti 131; tel: 06-322 981; www.gnam.beniculturali.it; Tue–Sun 8.30am–7.30pm; charge; map D3

Try hot or cold **Italian fast food** from the many eye-catching dishes at **Gargani**

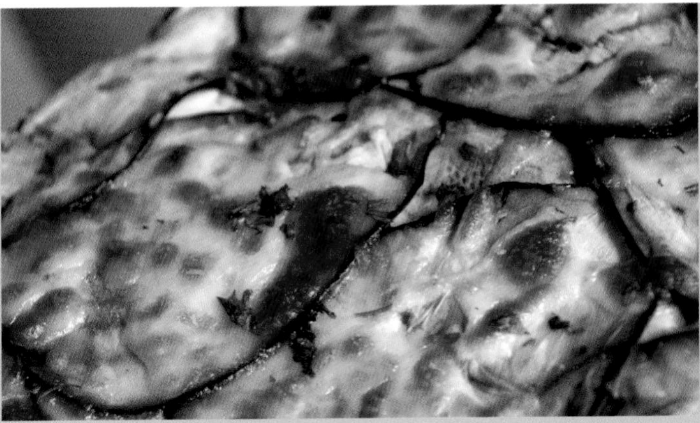

One quick glance reveals that Gastronomia Gargani is a neighbourhood delicatessen teeming with Italian speciality olive oils, expensive cheeses and designer pasta. A second look will reveal a polished *tavola calda*, hot food bar, where you hand-pick your lunch from freshly made mouth-watering dishes at a busy counter. Slices of roast veal, baked chicken, *polpette* (meatballs), home-made pastas and oven-baked fish are surrounded by grilled courgettes, aubergines, endive and Italian *insalate* (salads) such as *caprese* – mozzarella and sliced tomatoes.

It's an entirely civilised experience. You choose what you want by what is pleasing to the eye, and waiters transport your lunch to you, whether outside or inside at one of the wide wooden tables. Wine is served by the bottle and half bottle. If you are headed for a picnic at Villa Borghese, Gargani will pack your pickings to go.

Round off your lunch at the next-door **Bar Il Chicco**, a charming coffee bar that is always popular with local business men and women. Some say that it serves the best *sfogliatelle* – a shell-shaped layered pastry with ricotta cream – in the neighbourhood.

Gastronomia Gargani; via Lombardia 15; tel: 06-474 0865; Mon–Sat 7am–8pm; map E2

Go **Barberini bee-spotting** on a walk tracing the influence of a powerful Renaissance family

The noble Barberini dynasty were among Rome's greatest patrons of the arts. The family reached the height of its power in the 17th century when Cardinal Maffeo Barberini became Pope Urban VIII. Under his commission, artists turned the city into a showcase of Baroque. The family's coat of arms is three bees in a V-formation, and they decorate buildings and paintings all over the city. The Barberini first arrived from Florence in the late 16th century, where they went by the name Tafani (horsefly). They soon changed their name and out went the

unattractive old insect and in flew the ancient royal symbol of a bee.

To trace the bees, start at the hive, **Palazzo Barberini**. The family palace has part of the collection of the National Museum of Ancient Art. Highlights are Raphael's 1518 portrait of his lover, *La Fornarina* (the baker's daughter), Carvaggio's *Judith Slaying Holofernes* (1599) and *Henry VIII* by Holbein (1536).

Heading back down the slope to **Piazza Barberini** is Fontana del Tritone (1643), by Gianlorenzo Bernini, who had many commissions from the Barberini pope: the papal crest hides under the merman. In the north corner of Piazza Barberini is the Fontana delle Api, the Fountain of Bees *(pictured)*, a marble clam shell with three bees at its basin, designed by Bernini in 1644 as a gift from Urban VIII to the people.

Bees appear throughout the **Vatican Museums** *(p.72)*, in particular on the frescoed walls of the Gallery of Maps. There are also bees in **St Peter's Basilica** *(p.74)* on the *baldacchino* above the main altar and on Urban VIII's tomb in the apse to the right.

Stained-glass windows with bees illuminate the church of **Santa Maria in Ara Coeli** (map p.84 C5) on the Capitoline hill, and bees decorate the Borromini-designed **church of Sant'Ivo** (map p.25 F4) by Piazza Navona.

When you walk around Rome, look out not only for bees, but also for the Barberini sun, often appearing above the papal tiara. Also take a close look at the **Fontana della Barcaccia** on Piazza di Spagna *(p.52)*. On the inner part of the ship's bow, water streams from the mouth of a Barberini sun.

Palazzo Barberini, now the Galleria Nazionale d'Arte Antica; Via Barberini 18; tel: 06-482 4184; www.galleriaborghese.it; Tue–Sun 8.30am–7.30pm; charge; map E1

LA DOLCE VITA ON VIA VENETO

At the northern side of Piazza Barberini is the start of the Via Veneto (map E1–2) of *La Dolce Vita* fame. But the excitement that was once generated on the curving tree-lined street has now given way to nostalgia. Café and restaurant life caught by the flash of the 1960s paparazzi has been replaced with pricey brasseries, embassies and luxury hotels. A few of the infamous haunts are still open, such as **h club>Doney** at the Westin Excelsior (125) or **Harry's Bar** (150), as well as the new **La Ninfa Brasserie** at the Hotel Majestic (50) and the Boscolo Palace's **Cigar Bar** and café (70).

Take in **contemporary art and architecture** at **MAXXI**, Rome's newest architectural masterpiece

The MAXXI, National Museum of Art of the XXI Century, is more than a 10-year odyssey of its award-winning architect, Zaha Hadid. Throughout the 20th century, Rome relied on the past to hold its place in the international court of culture and high art, but in the 1990s it began encouraging competitions for new buildings.

The MAXXI is a three-level curved concrete box with its uppermost level weightlessly reaching skywards. The minimalist interior is a sensual maze of metal and cement waves pulsing through the galleries.

The MAXXI's collection represents acclaimed Italian and international artists with works from the 1960s onwards, and is Italy's first national museum dedicated to innovation in architecture as well as art. Part national museum, part private foundation, each year the MAXXI awards the Italian Prize for Contemporary Art, in a competition open to artists under 45 years of age and resident in Italy. Along with a cash prize, the winning artist's work becomes part of the permanent collection, rubbing shoulders with a roster of the contemporary art world's best and brightest, including Matthew Barney, Anselm Kiefer, Vic Muniz, Shahzia Sikander and Francesco Vezzoli.

A visit to the MAXXI can satisfy a quick contemporary art fix or be an all-day affair. The complex has an auditorium, library and media library specialising in art and architecture, bookshop, cafeteria, bar/restaurant and galleries for temporary exhibitions, performances and educational activities.

The large open square in front of the museum hosts artworks and live events, and the exterior walls are utilised for street art.

MAXXI; Via Guido Reni 10; tel: 06-321 0181; www.fondazionemaxxi.it; Tue–Sun 11am–7pm, Thur 11am–10pm; charge; Metro A to Flaminio, then tram 2 to the museum; map B4

Tune in to **high-fidelity sounds**, from classical to experimental jazz and rock, at the **Auditorium**

In 2002, the state-of-the-art Auditorium at Parco della Musica opened its halls to inaugurate a new era of music. Designed by Genoese architect Renzo Piano, the unconventional arts complex is made up of three scarab-shaped halls, or 'music boxes' as the architect calls them, which fan around an outdoor amphitheatre. The largest of the three halls, Santa Cecilia, is used for big orchestral concerts. The Sinipoli is smaller, and the Petrassi Hall is the smallest and most flexible. All have impeccable acoustics. Additional studios and multifunctional spaces are used for gallery shows, conferences and workshops.

On any day of the week, the 'city of music' resonates with the sounds of classical, jazz and pop concerts. It offers an excellent and varied programme from orchestral symphonies to performances by solo artists as diverse as Ute Lemper and Neil Young, alongside lesser-known talents.

In June and July, the music moves outside to Cavea, the amphitheatre, with concerts under the stars. And as a reminder of its ancient roots, the complex displays a 6th-century BC villa, unearthed during the Auditorium's construction.

The Auditorium's designer restaurant-bar **Red** (tel: 06-8069 1630) is all sweeping lines and elegant aesthetics, with red the predominant colour. Join the cognoscenti for a chic cocktail.

Auditorium Parco della Musica; Viale Pietro de Coubertin 30; tel 06-80241; www.auditorium.com; Metro A to Flamino, then bus/tram 2 to Piazza Apollodoro; map C4

LUCKY 13

Quirinale, Repubblica and Esquilino

Quirinale, Repubblica and Esquilino
0 100 200 300 400 500 m
0 100 200 300 400 500 yds
N
A
B
C
D
5
4
3
2
1
Largo di S. Susanna
S. Susanna
Piazza S. Bernar
Via S. N. da Tolentino
Via Barberini
BARBERINI
Fontana fel Tritone
Palazzo Barberini
Galleria Nazionale d' Arte Antica
V. lo Talentino
Via d. Quattro Fontane
Ministero d. Difesa
Via Rasella
V. del Traforo
Via dei Giardini
Palazzo d. Drago
Via Scuderie
d. Panetteria
GIARDINO DEL QUIRINALE
Quirinale
San Carlino
Via Modena
Museo Nazione delle Paste Alimentari
Sant'Andrea al Quirinale
Via del Quirinale
Palazzo del Quirinale (Presidential Palace)
Villa Spalletti Trivelli
Via Genova
Via A. Depre
Via Nazionale
Via della Dataria
Piacenza
Palazzo delle Esposizioni
S. Vitale
Piazza d Vimina
Piazza del Quirinale
Scuderie del Quirinale
Palazzo Consulta
Via della Consulta
Via Parma
Open Colonna
Via Genova
M.
Via XXIV Maggio
Tea Room
Via Palermo
Via Milano
Ministero dell' Interno
VILLA COLONNA
Palazzo Rospigliosi
Via del Boschetto
M. Viminale
Palazzo Colonna
Piazza dei SS. Apostoli
S. Silvestro
Via Nazionale
Via dei Serpenti
Istituto Chimico
Via IV Nov.
Banca d' Italia
Kokoro
Le Gallinelle
Via Cesa
Mazzarino
Panisperna
Piazza Venezia
Prefettura
Residenza Torre Colonna
Largo Magnanapoli
Villa Aldobrandini
Tre Scalini
God Save The Look
Urbana
Via Cimarra
Colonna Traiana
Mercati di Traiano
Via Panisperna
Agau
La Bottega del Caffè
Piazza Zingari
P.za Madonna dei Monti
Museo dei Fori Imperiali (Museum of Omperial Forums)
SS.Domenicani e Sisto
Pifebo Vintage
Fabio Picconi
Basilica Ulpia
V. di S. A. dei Goti
Al Vino Al Vino
Via degli Zingari
Largo Visconti Venosta
Via Alessandrina
Foro di Traiano
Inn at the Roman Forum
Via Leonina
CAVO
Foro di Augusto
Via T. de Conti
Via Baccina
Cavour
Via M.dei Monti
Via
Via dei Fori Imperiali
Piazza S.Pietro in Vincoli
San Pietro in Vincoli (St Peter in Chains)
Largo Corrado Ricci
Frangipane
Via d. Annibaldi
Via del Colosseo
Via del M. Oppio
Via delle T. di Tito
COLOSSEO
Domu Aurea Neror
Via N. Salvi
Colosseo
Piazza Colos

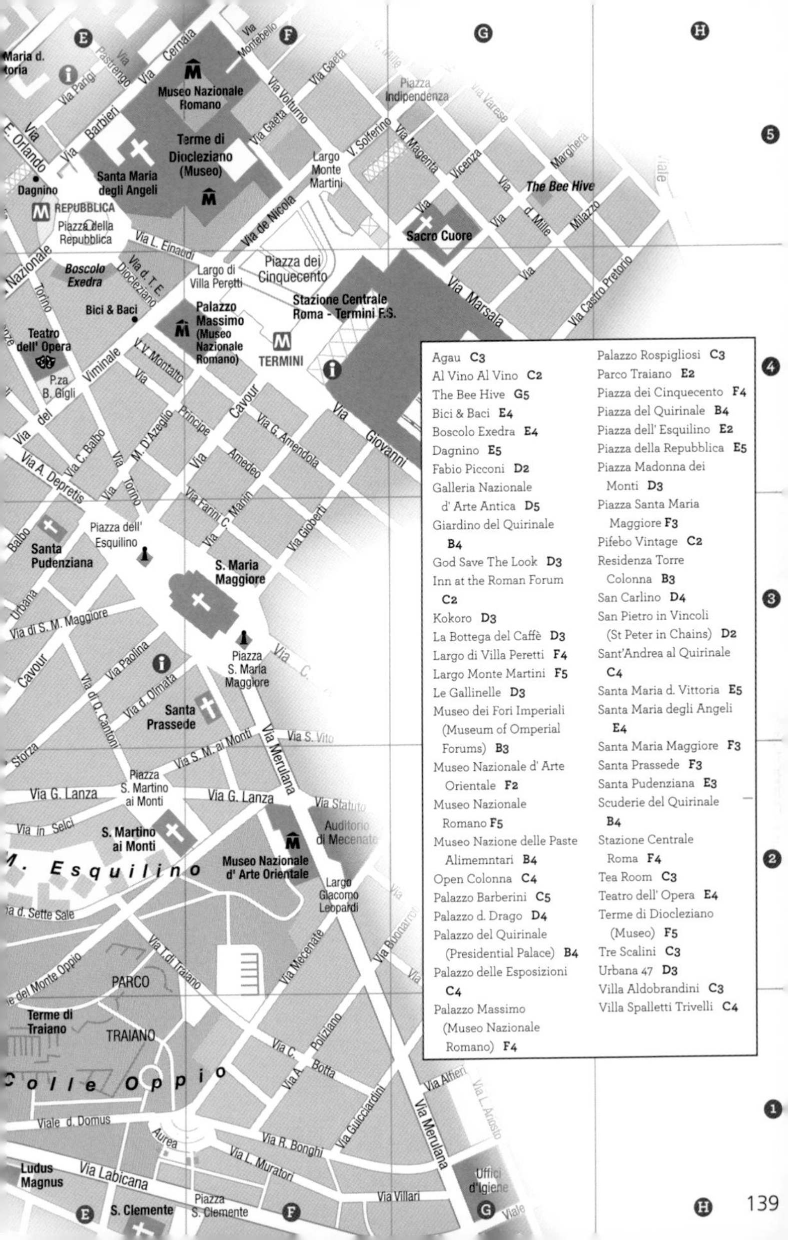

- Agau **C3**
- Al Vino Al Vino **C2**
- The Bee Hive **G5**
- Bici & Baci **E4**
- Boscolo Exedra **E4**
- Dagnino **E5**
- Fabio Picconi **D2**
- Galleria Nazionale d' Arte Antica **D5**
- Giardino del Quirinale **B4**
- God Save The Look **D3**
- Inn at the Roman Forum **C2**
- Kokoro **D3**
- La Bottega del Caffè **D3**
- Largo di Villa Peretti **F4**
- Largo Monte Martini **F5**
- Le Gallinelle **D3**
- Museo dei Fori Imperiali (Museum of Omperial Forums) **B3**
- Museo Nazionale d' Arte Orientale **F2**
- Museo Nazionale Romano **F5**
- Museo Nazione delle Paste Alimemntari **B4**
- Open Colonna **C4**
- Palazzo Barberini **C5**
- Palazzo d. Drago **D4**
- Palazzo del Quirinale (Presidential Palace) **B4**
- Palazzo delle Esposizioni **C4**
- Palazzo Massimo (Museo Nazionale Romano) **F4**
- Palazzo Rospigliosi **C3**
- Parco Traiano **E2**
- Piazza dei Cinquecento **F4**
- Piazza del Quirinale **B4**
- Piazza dell' Esquilino **E2**
- Piazza della Repubblica **E5**
- Piazza Madonna dei Monti **D3**
- Piazza Santa Maria Maggiore **F3**
- Pifebo Vintage **C2**
- Residenza Torre Colonna **B3**
- San Carlino **D4**
- San Pietro in Vincoli (St Peter in Chains) **D2**
- Sant'Andrea al Quirinale **C4**
- Santa Maria d. Vittoria **E5**
- Santa Maria degli Angeli **E4**
- Santa Maria Maggiore **F3**
- Santa Prassede **F3**
- Santa Pudenziana **E3**
- Scuderie del Quirinale **B4**
- Stazione Centrale Roma **F4**
- Tea Room **C3**
- Teatro dell' Opera **E4**
- Terme di Diocleziano (Museo) **F5**
- Tre Scalini **C3**
- Urbana 47 **D3**
- Villa Aldobrandini **C3**
- Villa Spalletti Trivelli **C4**

Watch the **changing of the presidential guard** at the **Quirinale Palace**

At precisely 3.15pm, Piazza del Quirinale comes to a halt as the city is regaled with the pomp of the changing of the honour guard in front of the Quirinale Palace, the grand office and residence of the president of Italy. Each afternoon, representatives from a single corps of Italy's armed forces parade in dress uniform and exchange watch with the existing guards. Sailors in the traditional white uniforms of the *Marina* salute the caped *carabinieri* (military police), and *Esercito* (army) representatives nod to *Aeronautica* (air force) counterparts. It can be a simple exchange of four servicemen, or an explosive parade with platoons and a marching band.

The honour guards then stand to attention in front of the Palace, a Baroque masterpiece built in 1583 as a papal summer residence and offices. With the fall of the Papal States, the creation of the Kingdom of Italy and foundation of the Republic, the Palace changed hands from popes to kings to presidents in less than 100 years.

On Sunday mornings the Quirinale Palace is open to the public who can walk through the majestic hallways and imagine themselves in charge. Don't miss the fresco over the stairs in the Great Hall, *Blessing Christ* by high Renaissance master Melozzo da Forlì *(p.72)*.

From October to June, afternoon concerts are held in the early 17th-century Pauline Chapel, which has a 20m-high vaulted ceiling covered in gilded molding. Visits to the 18th-century gardens are held on the 2nd and 4th Sunday of the month.

Changing of the Honour Guard; Mon–Sat 3.15pm, Sun and hols 4pm; Palazzo del Quirinale; Piazza del Quirinale; tel: 06-46991; www.quirinale.it; Sun 8.30am–noon; charge; map B4

Experience a **blockbuster art exhibition** at the **Scuderie del Quirinale**

Since 2000, the Scuderie has been wowing Rome and Italy with blockbuster exhibitions from all eras and genres of art. Some exhibitions have been part of the international circuit, while others like the popular Caravaggio show were specially designed and curated for the gallery.

The exhibition space occupies the second and third floors of the massive Scuderie (stables). The recently renovated halls perfectly light and display the exhibits. On the top floor is the glass-enclosed Great Window designed by architect Gae Aulenti as part of the renovation, and as the highest point of Rome's seven hills it has an amazing 180-degree view of the city.

The Scuderie are the former stables of the Quirinale Palace opposite, built in 1732 on the enormous 2nd-century AD Temple of Serapis. Traces of the temple wall can be seen on the road descending toward Trevi.

The sloping Piazza del Quirinale unites the two complexes. A 14m-high obelisk, from the Mausoleum of Augustus, stands at its centre above a fountain, flanked by two large statues of the Dioscuri – the horse tamers, Castor and Pollux. These 2nd-century statues are thought to be either from the Baths of Constantine, which lie beneath the square, or from a pediment on the Temple of Serapis.

The **Caffeteria Scuderie del Quirinale** (tel 06-6962 7221) on the mezzanine floor of the gallery has pastries and a hot bar selection, and views onto the piazza and city below.

Scuderie del Quirinale; Piazza del Quirinale; tel: 06-3996 7500; www.scuderiequirinale.it; Mon–Thur 9.30am–8pm, Fri until 11pm, Sat 9am–11pm, Sun until 10pm; charge; map B4

Swoon over Bernini's masterpiece, ***The Ecstasy of St Teresa***, at the church of Santa Maria della Vittoria

In Rome, you're never far from Bernini, the sculptor and architect who defined the Baroque city. However, to find one of his most elegant and sensual sculptures, *The Ecstasy of St Teresa*, takes a bit of hunting.

After the death of Urban VIII in 1644, Bernini found himself without papal support for the first time in his career. A Venetian cardinal stepped in and commissioned a new sculpture for his own tomb in Santa Maria della Vittoria, by Piazza della Repubblica. The work is a masterpiece of design and craftsmanship in which Bernini depicts St Teresa in the throes of divine glory as an angel pierces her repeatedly.

Teresa of Avila, who had just been canonised, described her ecstatic experience: 'I saw in his hand a long spear of gold, and at the iron's point there seemed to be a little fire. He appeared to me to be thrusting it at times into my heart, and to pierce my very entrails; when he drew it out, he seemed to draw them out also, and to leave me all on fire with a great love of God. The pain was so great, that it made me moan; and yet so surpassing was the sweetness of this excessive pain, that I could not wish to be rid of it.'

It is impossible not to equate the passion and pain of St Teresa with sexual pleasure, but Bernini captures the scene with his usual mastery. What makes this sculpture so divine is the setting he created: natural light beaming in through a concealed dome and a small window, and channelled onto the figures by gilded stucco rays from the heavens.

Santa Maria della Vittoria; Via XX Settembre 17; tel: 06-4274 0571; Mon–Sat 9am–noon, 3–6pm, Sun 3–6pm; map E5

Tootle around Rome on a Vespa like Audrey Hepburn and Gregory Peck in *Roman Holiday*

No cinematic moment encapsulates Rome better than that sunny morning in *Roman Holiday* when a gleeful Princess Ann (Audrey Hepburn) hops on the back of Joe Bradley's (Gregory Peck's) Vespa to joyride around the Eternal City. Grab your driving licence, pick out a scooter of choice and you too can feel the wind on your face on a *Roman Holiday* ride.

Vintage and contemporary Vespas and brand-new scooters are for hire at **Bici & Baci** ('bikes and kisses'). For those wanting a bit of history and who are looking to learn how to navigate Roman traffic, **Scooteroma** delivers your *motorino* to your door and will give you an hour-long, in-depth lesson in the fine art of scootering in the city. After your lesson, you follow behind the Scooter maven on your own vintage or modern scooter as she winds around the city. Or hop on the back of her 50cc scooter, *alla* Princess Ann, and enjoy being a back-seat driver in the world's most beautiful open-air museum.

Bici & Baci; Via del Viminale 5; tel: 06-482 8443; www.bicibaci.com; map E4; Scooteroma; tel: 338 822 7671; www.scooteroma.com

Browse the boutiques for one-of-a-kind finds in **Monti**, Rome's first neighbourhood

A city within a city, Monti is a microcosm of Rome. Despite recent gentrification, it stoically retains its inimitable personality. Its vibrant shopping and social scene is centuries old. In fact Monti was *Suburra* – 'under the city' – Ancient Rome's first neighbourhood of tenements teeming with plebians. Julius Caesar grew up here in a patrician family that had slipped down the rungs of the social ladder.

Today, a walk around Monti is a delightful tour of shops, cafés and restaurants. Designer boutiques and hip wine bars jockey with antique stores and small *trattorie*. Old-fashioned metal, mosaic and wood workshops still keep busy on the cobblestone streets, and children play football in the Piazza Madonna dei Monti, Monti's central square.

Point your compass north and begin crisscrossing in and around the area between Via dei Serpenti and Via Urbana for Monti's best outlets. Running almost a straight north-south, Via dei Serpenti is lined with shops. At 25 is **Agau**, an exclusive and modern jewellery store. Not far away is neighbourhood *enoteca* **Al Vino** (19; tel: 06-485803), a small and casual wine bar with a large selection of wines, grappas, whiskeys, cheeses and *salumi*, and some traditional Italian dishes. **Pifebo Vintage** (141) is stocked with grandma's knick-knacks for you to rummage through.

Running parallel to Via dei Serpenti, is Via del Boschetto dotted with funky shops. **Le Gallinelle** (76) is one of Rome's vintage headquarters. Take some time to peruse the mixed bag of new and classic items. Next door, **Kokoro** (75) shows off its one-of-a-kind dresses and leather belts and bags. Down the street at 34, **The Tea Room** is a tiny club full of hipsters, musicians, artists and

LIFE IN THE SQUARE

Piazza Madonna dei Monti is a constant procession of activity around its fountain. All day there is movement, from the morning pram pushers and dog walkers and the elderly women feeding pigeons, to the afternoon kids playing soccer against the church door, and music students strumming guitars at dusk. Take a front-row seat at **La Bottega del Caffè** (tel: 06-4741 578; map D3) just behind the fountain. Open until the wee hours, La Bottega serves every beverage and booze, from good cappuccinos to wickedly strong cocktails. There's also a charming café menu of pastries, antipasti, pastas and salads.

wannabees listening to music and enjoying drinking and dancing into the early hours of the morning. **Fabio Picconi** (148) is a bohemian rhapsody of vintage costume jewellery.

Heading uphill and perpendicular to Boschetto is Via Panisperna where the historic, rustic **Tre Scalini** wine bar (251; tel: 06-4890 7495) resides. It's always crowded, so arrive early. Keep going up the hill to **God Save the Look** (227A), another of Monti's many vintage shops.

Last but definitely not least is Via Urbana, with a peppering of cafés, food stores, shoe shops, clothing stores, baby boutiques and grocers. Monti's eternally hip hang out at **Urbana 47** (47; tel: 06-4788 4006), an all-day coffee and wine shop, which has a lunch and dinner menu of dishes made with local organic ingredients.

Via dei Serpenti, Via del Boschetto C3
Via Panisperna C3–D3
Via Urbana D3–E3

Tell the time using the sun's rays inside the Basilica of **St Mary of the Angels**

The Basilica di Santa Maria degli Angeli (St Mary of the Angels) hides behind the rough walls of the early 4th-century Baths of Diocletian. In 1561, the church was developed in the remaining walls of the bath complex. Plans were overseen by several architects including Michelangelo, and the result is a mellifluous fusion of classic architecture and late Renaissance design.

The entrance of the church is the remnants of the bath's *caldarium*. Walk through the doors and you are pushed into a spectacular transept *(pictured)* with pink granite columns, eight from the original bath. On a diagonal from the far right corner is a bronze meridian line, inlaid in the floor in 1703 to check the accuracy of the Gregorian calendar. Sunlight shines through a small hole in the wall, casting light on the line, which in turn tells the time. The meridian was used to synchronise Rome's bell towers, later replaced by the noon cannon fire from the Gianicolo.

Outside, the majestic Piazza della Repubblica, with the charmingly erotic Fountain of the Naiads, was once the great terrace of the Baths of Diocletian.

Just across the piazza on Via V. Emanuele Orlando is the entrance to the Galleria Esedra where **Dagnino** (tel: 06-481 8660; map E5) is a wonderful Sicilian gourmet *caffeteria* and pastry shop, known for its delicious *casatine* (ricotta and almond pastries), *arancine* (stuffed deep-fried rice balls), *gelato al brioche* (ice cream in a brioche), wine selection and Mariage Frères teas.

Santa Maria degli Angeli; Piazza della Repubblica; tel: 06-488 0812; Mon–Sat 7am–6.30pm, Sun until 7.30pm; map E5

Immerse yourself in the grandeur of a Roman bathhouse at the **Baths of Diocletian**

The Baths of Diocletian were the largest of the imperial *thermae*, covering 11 hectares in the area now known as Piazza della Repubblica. Although traces can be seen in the perimeter of the piazza and in the Basilica of Santa Maria degli Angeli *(left)*, to experience the grandeur of the baths you must visit the museum.

Hidden behind the church, on Via Enrico de Nicola the Terme di Diocleziano museum is one of the four sites of the Museo Nazionale Romano *(p.150)*. The garden entrance is decorated with Roman tombs and statuary and lined with a gravel path, which leads to the museum entrance.

The museum is spread over two structures. The first is the cloister *(pictured)*, attributed to Michelangelo and displaying the epigraphy collection, which chronicles the history of the empire through ancient artefacts. The second structure is the main hall, part of the ancient bath complex.

Head for the southwest corner to the rectangular hall, a vestibule that led to the baths' changing rooms. The surrounding 28m-high walls provide an instant idea of the greatness of these baths. Inside the hall are reconstructed tombs found in and around the city, including the enormous Platorini family tomb, from 18 BC, a house-size brick structure with marble detail. After the tombs, visit the epigraphic collection on the 1st floor and test your Latin skills on the slave collar that reads: 'If lost, please return to...'

Museo Nazionale Romano, Terme di Diocleziano; Via Enrico de Nicola 79; tel: 06-3996 7700; Tue–Sun 9am–7.45pm; charge; map F5

Investigate the **two giants of Baroque Rome** on an **architectural walk** along the Via del Quirinale

One of the great rivalries of 17th-century Rome was between the neurotic but inventive Francesco Borromini and the charming and successful Gianlorenzo Bernini *(pictured)*, and there is no better place to compare the styles of these masters of Baroque than two churches on Via del Quirinale.

San Carlo alle Quattro Fontane, known as San Carlino, gets its name from the four fountains at each corner of the crossroads at the highest point of the Quirinal Hill. In 1641, Borromini unveiled his new church here. A masterpiece in miniature, what immediately grabs your attention is its dynamic, undulating facade. The compressed interior is a narrow oval, with four surrounding enclaves weaving in and out. A sublime light travels through the tiny cupola and dome, whose only decoration is white moulding and coffering. To the right of the altar is a door and hallway that leads to Borromini's equally harmonious cloister.

Down the street at Via del Quirinale 29 is **Sant'Andrea al Quirinale**, Bernini's 1661 response to Borromini's masterpiece. A smooth arcing facade with a simple double column entrance, Sant'Andrea is outwardly minimal in comparison. The oval interior, elliptical across its width, is a different matter. Whereas San Carlino is a study in white on white, Sant'Andrea is a celebration of decoration, with gold and bronze gilding rampant in its chapels. Transcendental it is not, exulting it is.

San Carlo; Via del Quirinale 23; tel: 06-488 3109; Mon–Fri 10am–1pm, 3–6pm, Sat 10am–1pm, Sun noon–1pm; map D4
Sant'Andrea al Quirinale; Via del Quirinale 29; tel: 06-474 0807; Wed–Fri 8am–noon, 4–7pm; map D4

Celebrate **cutting-edge art and cuisine** at the **Palazzo delle Esposizioni**

Halfway down the Via Nazionale is the neoclassical Palazzo delle Esposizioni, a turn-of-the-century exhibition hall and now cutting-edge venue for blockbuster shows. With more than 10,000 square metres of gallery space, the palazzo is a hub for Rome's largest cultural events. Reopened in 2007 with an explosive Mark Rothko retrospective, it has since been showcasing artists, photographers and film-makers, including Giorgio di Chirico, Bill Viola and Stanley Kubrick, alongside extravaganzas like the smash hit Darwin exhibition.

The palazzo experience is multi-medial and multidisciplinary. Perusing the calendar, you'll find weekly films, lectures by international critics in the 90-seat auditorium, and programmes for children in the *laboratorio*. The street-level Bookàbar bookshop has a broad selection of art books and books for children, while the garden Bookàbar café is the place for a quick coffee and fresh air.

Brunch or dine at **Open Colonna** (Scalinata di Via Milano 9a; tel: 06-4782 2641; closed Mon; *pictured*), celebrity chef Antonello Colonna's restaurant on the uppermost level of the Palazzo. His creative 'modern Italian' cuisine in a gorgeous glassed-in room with modern design is worthy of its one Michelin star. For snacks and light fare, try the Open Panino, his newly invented sandwich – an egg frittata on Rosetta bun with *cipolline* onions, olive oil and pancetta (bacon). Slip up to the Terrace Bar to toast the moonlight.

Palazzo delle Esposizioni; Via Nazionale 194; tel: 06-482 8760; www.palazzoesposizioni.it; Tue–Thur, Sun 10am–8pm, Fri, Sat 10am–10.30pm; map C4

Study **1st-century frescoes of a garden paradise** from the villa of Empress Livia at **Palazzo Massimo**

Although the Palazzo Massimo contains four floors filled with artefacts, from coins and statuary to mosaics and marble friezes, when you arrive you should head straight to the wonderful frescoes on the top floor.

The first low-lit room has a beautifully detailed 1st-century fresco from the Villa of Livia, wife of the Emperor Augustus, in Prima Porta, a northern suburb of Rome. The decorative theme for the villa's subterranean *triclinium* (dining room) was a garden setting. Lifelike birds on the boughs of pomegranate trees and ornamental plants in a sunny grove created a perpetual spring in the underground room.

Around the corner are rooms from Augustan General Agrippa's family villa. The winter dining room is exceptional – an almost entirely black fresco with flowers and a detailed narrative frieze. The idea of the black background was that it would absorb the sun's rays and heat the room during the cold months. Also outstanding are the three *cubicula* (bedrooms) with figurative stucco ceilings.

Museo Nazionale Romano, Palazzo Massimo; Largo di Villa Peretti 1; tel: 06-4890 3500; www.archeoroma.com; Tue–Sun 9am–7.45pm; map F4

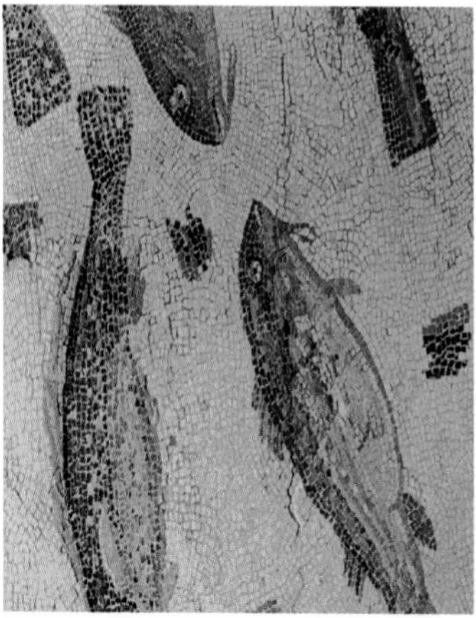

NATIONAL ROMAN MUSEUMS

The Museo Nazionale Romano scheme was started in 1890 in order to collect together all the antiquarian objects in the city from the 5th century BC to the 3rd century AD. A ticket to the Palazzo Massimo also gives you access over three days to the **Baths of Diocletian** *(p.147)*; **Palazzo Altemps** (Piazza di Sant'Apollinare 48; tel: 06-3996 700; map p.25 E5), a delightful museum set around a courtyard with many treasures of classical statuary and art; and **Crypta Balbi** (Via delle Botteghe Oscure 31; tel: 06-678 0167; map p.25 G2), with a theatre and an early medieval museum.

See *La Bohème* in style from the gilded boxes of the **Teatro dell'Opera**

If Venice's La Fenice, Milan's La Scala and Naple's San Carlo are the three top stops on Italy's Opera Grand Tour, Rome's Teatro dell'Opera is a deserving *intermezzo*. The 1,600-seat opera house has undergone several reincarnations from its original conception as Teatro Constanzi, designed in 1879 by Achille Sfondrini, a theatre specialist from Milan. Purchased in 1929 by the civic administration of Rome, it had three subsequent facelifts. Though the exterior of Teatro dell'Opera lacks the grandeur of its compatriots, its interior will not disappoint anyone looking for opera chic.

Sitting in the Teatro dell'Opera is like being inside a Fabergé egg. Four tiers of arcaded boxes line the horseshoe-shaped theatre and glow under the ceiling dome – a monumental fresco of a pastoral scene surrounding the centre chandelier 6m in diameter and composed of 27,000 crystal drops. Art Nouveau moulding and delicate lighting fixtures decorate the walls, boxes and gallery seats.

Rome's opera season begins in October and carries through to the end of May, with performances by both the Opera and Corps de Ballet. Well respected and a well-known participant in the international opera scene, the Teatro dell'Opera has a creative seasonal programme with opera favourites such as *Madame Butterfly* and *Tosca*, as well as avant-garde performances like *Falstaff* staged by Zeffirelli.

Many great conductors have worked with the resident Orchestra del Teatro dell'Opera, and there is a chorus of 90. In July and August, the Teatro dell'Opera moves its opera and ballet performances to the auspicious Baths of Caracalla *(p.159)*.

Teatro dell'Opera; Piazza Beniamino Gigli 7; tel: 06-4816 0255; www.operaroma.it; map E4

Admire late Roman mosaics and Michelangelo's *Moses* on a **walking tour of Esquilino's churches**

The Esquilino neighbourhood is a treasure trove of beautiful, ancient churches associated with St Paul and the first popes, with even more beautiful and ancient artwork inside.

Starting from the top is the **Basilica di Santa Maria Maggiore** (Via Liberiana 27; map F3), the largest church devoted to the Virgin Mary, and temporary home to the popes on their return from Avignon. The mosaics above the columns in the nave depicting stories form the Old Testament are exceptional, and the decoration is complemented by the powerful apse mosaic of *The Coronation of the Virgin* (1295) by Jacopo Torriti. The expansive wood-coffered basilica ceiling was added in the 1490s and decorated with what is said to be the first gold brought from the New World, donated by Ferdinand and Isabella of Spain. In the reliquary crypt, below the high altar, are the supposed relics of Jesus's Manger from Bethlehem.

Across the street in Via di Santa Prassede 9/a, don't let the plain entrance to the **church of Santa Prassede** (map F3) fool you. Inside is a sparkling gem of 9th-century mosaics built for Pope Paschal I. Jesus sits in the centre of the main altar with St Paul and St Peter, accompanied by St Prassede and her sister Pudenziana in whose father's house St Peter

reportedly stayed. On the far left is a mosaic of 9th-century Pope Paschal I, holding a model of the church, which he enlarged. Symbols of the Apostles decorate the arch, centred on a lamb above a throne, representing Christ.

On the right of the aisle is the small Chapel of St Zeno. The richly coloured ceiling vault is magnificent, depicting a Christ held aloft by four angels on a luscious gold background, all in mosaic glass tiles. On the right-hand wall is one of Rome's legendary relics – a fragment of the Column of The Flagellation, where Christ was chained. The original main entrance of the church leads to a tiny medieval courtyard with apartments built into the walls.

Return to Santa Maria Maggiore, and walk down to Via Urbana to the tiny sister **church of Santa Pudenziana** (Via Urbana 160; map E3; *pictured*), the oldest place of Christian worship in Rome and home of the earliest popes. The late Roman mosaics have had several bouts of questionable restoration, but the scene in the apse of the Apostles in Roman togas is mesmerising.

Head down Via Cavour to Via San Franscecso Di Paola, where a staircase on the left will take you to Piazza San Pietro in Vincoli. The **church of St Peter in Chains** (Piazza San Pietro in Vincoli 4a; map D2) is for Michelangelo lovers, who come in search of his *Moses*. More than 2m of warm Carrara marble, *Moses* is seated, with horns and a magnificent beard. The statue was made for the tomb of Pope Julius II, a member of the della Rovere family whose church this was. After the sculpture, enjoy the frescoes in the apse and the della Rovere oak tree symbols, then step down into the shrine to see the chains that supposedly bound St Peter. Tradition says they were miraculously rejoined after his death.

VINTAGE TRAM RIDES

Rome's public transport provider, ATAC, has refurbished several early 20th-century trams which can be boarded on regular runs, or hired for special occasions. A weekly vintage tram has a city tour starting at Piazza Porta Maggiore, near Termini Station. Risto-trams are Belle Epoque style with elegant dining tables; TramJazz, in a 1947 Stanga tramcar, has live jazz; and in the 1928 TramBelcanto you can hear opera favourites. Trips last around three hours. Information: tel: 339 633 4700; www.trambus.com or www.atac.roma.it.

Aventino, Testaccio and Piramide

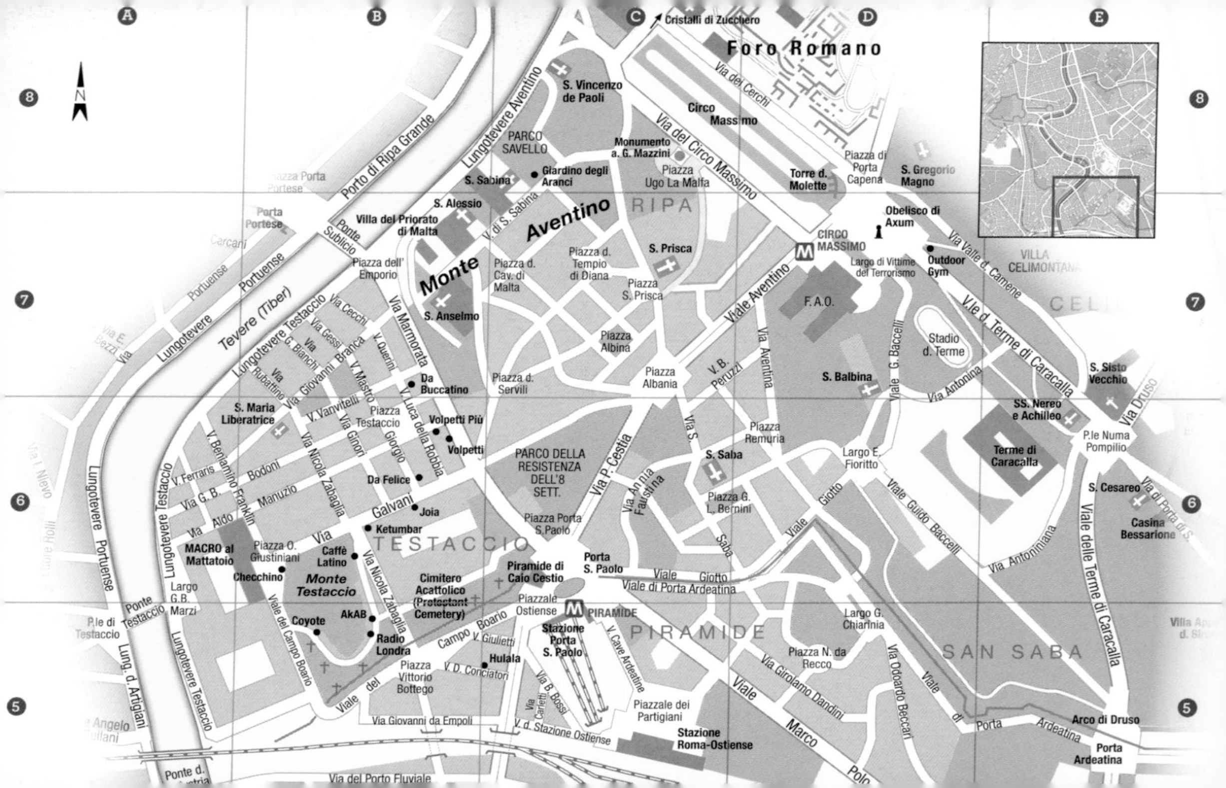
Foro Romano
Cristalli di Zucchero
Circo Massimo
Via dei Cerchi
Via del Circo Massimo
S. Vincenzo de Paoli
PARCO SAVELLO
Giardino degli Aranci
Monumento a. G. Mazzini
Piazza Ugo La Malfa
S. Sabina
S. Alessio
Villa del Priorato di Malta
V. di S. Sabina
Aventino
RIPA
Monte
S. Anselmo
Piazza d. Cav. di Malta
Piazza d. Tempio di Diana
S. Prisca
Piazza S. Prisca
Piazza Albina
Piazza Albania
Piazza d. Servili
Torre d. Molette
Piazza di Porta Capena
S. Gregorio Magno
Obelisco di Axum
CIRCO MASSIMO
Largo di Vittime del Terrorismo
Outdoor Gym
Via Valle d. Camene
VILLA CELIMONTANA
F.A.O.
Viale Aventino
Via Aventina
V. B. Peruzzi
Stadio d. Terme
V.le d. Terme di Caracalla
Viale G. Baccelli
S. Balbina
Via Antonina
S. Sisto Vecchio
Via Druso
SS. Nereo e Achilleo
P.le Numa Pompilio
Terme di Caracalla
Largo E. Fioritto
Viale Guido Baccelli
Via Antoniniana
S. Cesareo
Casina Bessarione
Via di Porta di S.
Viale delle Terme di Caracalla
Villa Appia d. Sirene
Porto di Ripa Grande
Piazza Porta Portese
Porta Portese
Carcani
Portuense
Lungotevere Portuense
Tevere (Tiber)
Lungotevere Aventino
Ponte Sublicio
Piazza dell' Emporio
Lungotevere Testaccio
Via Cecchi
Via Gessi
Via G. Bianchi
Via Rubattino
Via Giovanni Branca
V. Querini
V. Mastro
Via Marmorata
Da Buccatino
V. Luca della Robbia
Volpetti Più
Volpetti
Piazza Testaccio
Giorgio
Via Ginori
V. Vanvitelli
S. Maria Liberatrice
V. Beniamino Franklin
V. Ferraris
Via G. B. Bodoni
Via Aldo Manuzio
Via Nicola Zabaglia
Da Felice
Galvani
Joia
Ketumbar
Via
TESTACCIO
PARCO DELLA RESISTENZA DELL'8 SETT.
Via P. Cestia
Piazza Porta S.Paolo
Piazza Remuria
Via S. Saba
S. Saba
Piazza G. L. Bernini
Via Annia Faustina
Viale Giotto
MACRO al Mattatoio
Piazza O. Giustiniani
Caffè Latino
Checchino
Monte Testaccio
Cimitero Acattolico (Protestant Cemetery)
Piramide di Caio Cestio
Porta S. Paolo
Viale di Porta Ardeatina
Largo G.B. Marzi
Ponte Testaccio
P.le di Testaccio
Lung. d. Artigiani
Via del Campo Boario
Coyote
AkAB
Radio Londra
Piazzale Ostiense
PIRAMIDE
Campo Boario
V. Giulietti
Hulala
V. D. Conciatori
Piazza Vittorio Bottego
Viale del
Stazione Porta S. Paolo
V. Cave Ardeatine
Via B. Bossi
Via Carletti
PIRAMIDE
Largo G. Chiarinia
Piazza N. da Recco
Via Girolamo Dandini
Via Odoardo Beccari
SAN SABA
Viale di Porta Ardeatina
Arco di Druso
Porta Ardeatina
Piazzale dei Partigiani
Stazione Roma-Ostiense
Viale Marco Polo
Via Giovanni da Empoli
V. d. Stazione Ostiense
Via del Porto Fluviale
Ponte d.
Via I. Nievo
Via E. Bezzi
CELI
N
A
B
C
D
E
8
7
6
5

Arco di Druso **E5**
Caffè Latino **B6**
Checchino **B6**
Cimitero Acattolico (Protestant Cemetery) **B6**
Cinema-Teatro Palladium **C2**
Circo Massimo **C8**
Coyote **B5**
Cristalli di Zucchero **C8**
Da Felice **B6**
Da Buccatino **B7**
Dar Moschino **C2**
EUR **B1**
Giardino degli Aranci **C8**
Hulala **C5**
Joia **B6**
Ketumbar **B6**
MACRO al Mattatoio **A6**
Monte Testaccio **B6**
Monumento a. G. Mazzini **C8**
Museo della Centrale Montemartini **B4**
Obelisco di Axum **D7**
Ostia Antica **B1**
Outdoor Gym **D7**
Parco Savello **C8**
Piazza B. Romana **C2**
Piazza Oderico da Pordenone **E2**
Piazza Testaccio **B6**
Piazzale Ostiense **C6**
Piramide di Caio Cestio **C6**
Radio Londra **B5**
S. Isidoro **D2**
Terme di Caracalla **E6**
Villa del Priorato di Malta **B7**
Volpetti **B6**
Volpetti Più **B6**

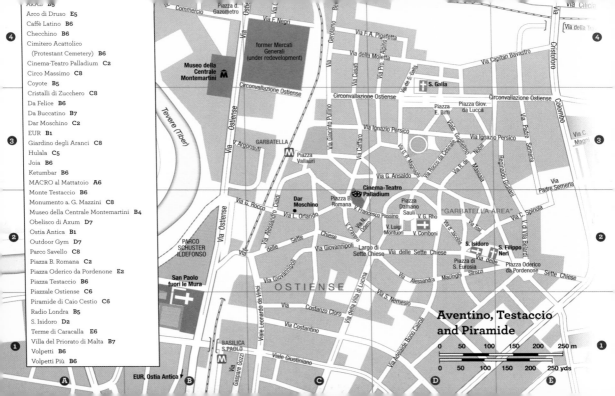

Aventino, Testaccio and Piramide

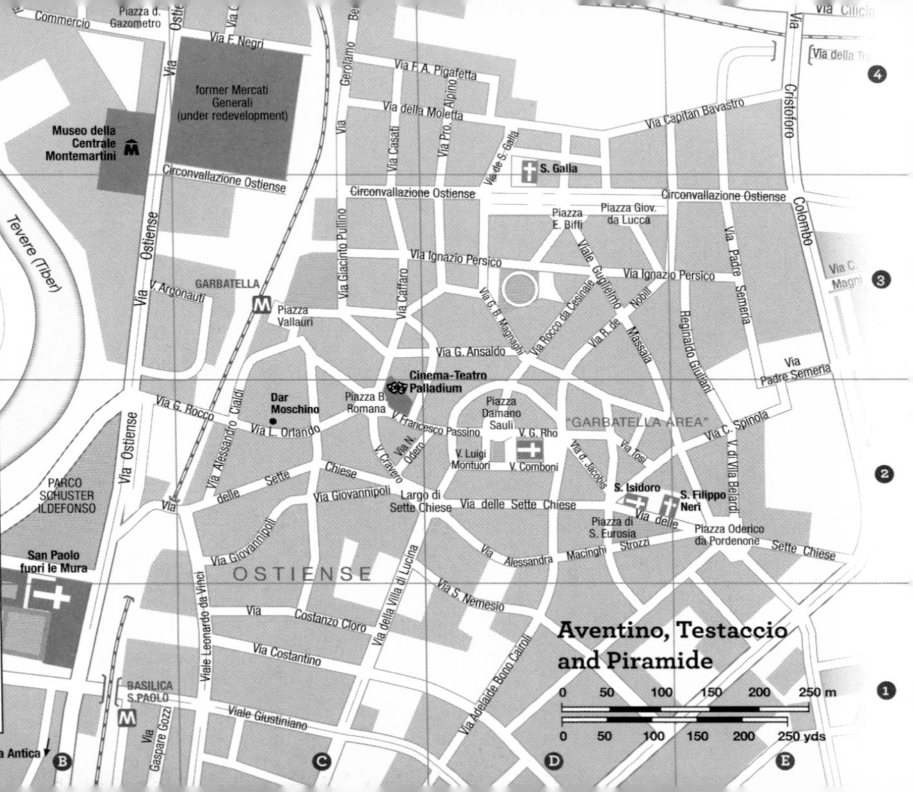

Enjoy a **picnic under orange trees** on the aristocratic heights of **Aventine Hill**

The Aventino is one of the seven hills of Rome, and it has been inhabited by patrician families since the age of the Republic. A lordly feeling is retained in its leafy streets and walled gardens.

To reach the hill, follow the Via D. Greca up from the Bocca della Verità at the church of Santa Maria in Cosmedin *(p. 91)*, and take the first right, the ancient Roman road Clivo dei Publicii, continuing steeply uphill and turning right onto Via di Santa Sabina. Walk along a brick wall to the entrance of the Parco Savello, marked by a whimsical, early Baroque fountain with a large mask by Giacomo della Porta.

The former grounds of a 13th-century fortress are an inspiration for romance and ideal for a picnic. The park was designed in 1932 by Raffaelle del Vico and is known as the Giardino degli Aranci after its many colourful and manicured orange trees. Wander through to the terrace. This dramatic vantage point gives a postcard-perfect panorama from the rooftops of Trastevere to the Capitoline hill.

Next door is the **church of Santa Sabina**, a popular wedding location. It has a simple 5th-century interior, and the cypress wood doors on the left as you enter date from the 420s and have one of the earliest depictions of the crucifixion.

From here the road leads into **Piazza dei Cavalieri di Malta** (Knights of Malta) and the Priorato di Malta. Founded in 1050, this chivalric order continues to operate as a charity. Peek through the keyhole in the doorway and you'll see the faraway dome of St Peter's appear as if it were in the garden.

Giardino degli Aranci or Parco Savello; Via di Santa Sabina; daily 7am–7pm; map C8

Watch **opera under the stars** at the **Baths of Caracalla** where the Three Tenors sang

Since 1937, the Baths of Caracalla have been diverting visitors in summer, when the heat makes Rome almost unforgivable. The monumental ruins of this 3rd-century AD bathhouse are the stage and scenery for the Teatro dell'Opera summer season, which delivers an inimitable musical experience under the stars, scented by umbrella pines.

The *thermae* were a public baths extending over 13 hectares. Essentially a leisure emporium, they satisfied the desires of its thousands of daily visitors in its pools, saunas, sports ground, running track, salons, shops, schools and library. Its main building, 228m long, 116m wide and 38.5m high, is a picturesque ruin of arches and crumbling walls that acts as a stage.

Caracalla is noted for its grand opera, ballets, and musical masterpieces including the 1990 Three Tenors concert with Luciano Pavarotti, Jose Carreras and Placido Domingo. Performances begin at dusk, as the sun sets on the red-brick walls and the orchestra tunes.

Have a €5 note in your pocket for a slice of *cocomero* (watermelon) to eat on your way home. One of Rome's favourite watermelon sellers stands in front of the **Circus Maximus** *(p.99)* on Viale Aventino and Piazza di Porta Capena and stays open into the night.

Teatro dell'Opera, Terme di Caracalla; Viale delle Terme di Caracalla; tel: 06-4816 0255; www.operaroma.it; June–Aug; map E6

Pay homage to the Romantic poets **Keats and Shelley** at the **Protestant Cemetery**

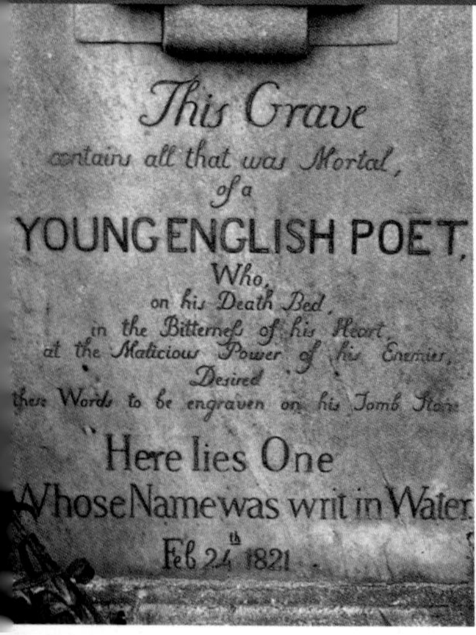

The Protestant Cemetery, officially called the Cimitero Acattolico, is the final resting place of the Romantic poets John Keats and Percy Bysshe Shelley. Founded in 1734 as the burial ground for all non-Catholics, it contains many British, German, Scandinavian, Russian and American artistic and diplomatic figures as well as Goethe's son August and Antonio Gramsci, father of Italian Marxism.

Ashes, such as Shelley's, are here as well as bones – it was not until 1963 that the pope lifted the Catholic Church's ban on cremation. A few years before he drowned, Shelley wrote, 'It might make one in love with death, to think that one should be buried in so sweet a place.'

Nestled on a hill beside the Pyramid of Caius Cestius, the cemetery is a cypress-filled haven that offers a snapshot of expat life and death in the city – this is where Henry James's fictional Daisy Miller came to rest after catching 'Roman Fever'.

Bordered by high walls, the front gate can be found on Via Caio Cestio where ringing the bell gains you admittance. Once inside, take a stroll in this peaceful atmosphere as you make out the names on the gravestones.

Neglected and in disrepair for many years, the site was added to the World Monument Fund's 2006 list of the 100 Most Endangered Sites. The Friends of the Non-Catholic Cemetery in Rome has been founded to help with conservation, and a money box is located near the exit if you have spare coins and wish to help.

Cimitero Acattolico; Via Caio Cestio 6; tel: 06-574 1900; www.protestantcemetery.it; Mon–Sat 9am–1pm, Sun and hols 9am–1pm; free; Metro B to Piramide; map B6

Step inside a **Roman pyramid** for a private glimpse at 1st-century BC frescoes

You may well pass by Rome's pyramid during your visit and wonder why it is there. It was erected in 12 BC as a tomb for Gaius Cestius, a magistrate with a penchant for all things Egyptian, following the conquest of Upper Egypt in 30 BC. Built to look like the pyramids of Giza, it has a long, narrow entrance corridor and a small barrel-vaulted chamber decorated with exquisite frescoes.

Ever since its creation, the pyramid has stopped traffic. In the 3rd century, facing potential barbarian invasion as the city's fortunes waned, the Romans incorporated the pyramid into the city walls. It became one of the essential sights of the Grand Tour, inspiring writers and painters like Rubens, Poussin and Lallemand. There are severely restricted visiting hours. Individual tours take place at precisely 11am on the 2nd and 4th Saturday of each month, are conducted in Italian and require reservation. English-language tours are only available for groups. Regardless of language, the pyramid is worth the visit.

Piramide; Piazzale Ostiense; tel: 06-3996 7700; www.060608.it; Metro B to Piramide; map C6

A FANCY FOR OBELISKS

Ancient Rome had a fascination with Egyptology, 'importing' obelisks to decorate the city. Eight of them are prominently visible in piazzas. The oldest and largest at 45m is found in front of the Basilica di San Giovanni in Laterano *(map p.85 H2)*, brought down the Nile and shipped to Rome by Constantius II. Rome also has at least five 2nd-century copies of originals, and five modern versions including Mussolini's at the entrance to the Olympic Stadium. An obelisk taken by Mussolini from Ethiopia in 1937 and erected in Piazza di Porta Capena was returned in 2005.

Taste **authentic Roman cuisine** in the former slaughterhouse district at **Checchino dal 1887**

The Testaccio neighbourhood is the city's former slaughterhouse district and home to one of Rome's landmark restaurants, Checchino dal 1887. Here, the Mariani family has been serving a bewitching array of traditional Roman gastronomy like *coda alla vaccinara* (oxtail stew), *spaghetti alla gricia* (pecorino cheese, bacon and olive oil) and *fagioli e cotiche* (beans and pork rinds) for five generations. Try their fragrant finger burners, *costolette d'abbacchio alla scottadito.* These spit-roasted baby lamb chops are eaten in your fingers, which is unusual in a city where formality requires that pizza be eaten with a knife and fork.

In spite of its humble cuisine, Checchino's is elegant and has a clientele of journalists, politicians and slow-food connoisseurs. The building started life as a wine house, selling to the local butchers. Have a look at their impressive cellar, filled with more than 600 wines from all over the world, as well as older vintages of Italian classics and little-known regional gems. The bottles arrayed along the carved-out amphora-shard walls of the 2,000-year-old Monte dei Cocci are an experience not to be missed.

For a modern spin on a Roman classic, go to **Da Felice** (Via Maestro Giorgio 29; tel: 06-574 6800; closed Sun; map B6). Try traditional *cacio e pepe* (pecorino cheese and ground pepper) and *tiramisù al bicchiere* (tiramisù in a glass). Tables at this attractive tiled restaurant should be reserved well in advance, since it's a noted Michelin Bib Gourmand.

For something simpler, hang out with Roma football club at **Da Bucatino** (Via Luca della Robbia 84; tel: 06-574 6886; map B7) and enjoy home-made pastas.

Checchino dal 1887; Via di Monte; tel: 06-574 6318; Tue–Sat L and D; map B6

Take home **foodie delights**, including top-quality Italian salami and cheese, at **Volpetti**

TESTACCIO MARKET
Take a stroll through Testaccio Market's narrow corridors where 50 vendors offer cheese, meats, fish and mounds of seasonal fruits and vegetables including local delicacies like *puntarelle* (tender young chicory shoots). One stall not to be missed is the tomato vendor, with a cheery display of more than 30 varieties, from regional specialities to classics. Picking the perfect tomato requires three essential senses – touch, smell and taste – but market etiquette means no touching, so let the vendors help you. But first ask if you can sample a slice.

Cheeses and pastries and breads, oh my! Volpetti is often the main reason to come to Testaccio. It is Rome's very best *salumeria,* a delicatessen focusing on cured meats. Choose from more than a dozen different prosciutto like the sweet *San Daniele,* and more than 30 *salsicce*, from soft, spreadable *ciauscolo* to *cinghiale* (wild boar sausages) and *capocollo* (salami from Calabria).

A range of Italian cheeses includes old favourites ricotta (freshly made goat's cheese), mozzarella and *burrata* as well as medieval Toma from Piedmont and *pecorino sotto cenere* (cheese seasoned under ash). Everything is available to sample. Bread is made daily, and staff will create the perfect *panino* for your picnic.

Wines, oils, condiments and desserts are also available, and if ordering a takeaway, taste the *alici marinati* (marinated anchovies). Volpetti will vacuum-pack truffles, sausages, cheeses and prosciutto on request.

For those wanting to sit, head around the corner to **Volpetti Pìu** (Via Alessandro Volta 8; tel: 06-574 4306; closed Sun; map B6), Volpetti's 'experimental fast food' restaurant of pastas, soups, meat dishes, vegetables and desserts.

Volpetti; Via Marmorata 47; tel: 06-5742 3520; www.volpetti.com; Mon–Sat 8am–2pm, 5–8.15pm; map B6

Size up an **ancient mosaic** in a former power plant at the **Centrale Montemartini** museum

Almost unknown to the general public, the Museo della Centrale Montemartini is an extraordinary example of Rome's new movement in cultural mélange where the old and the new are showcased together. The Centrale Montemartini was Rome's first power station, built in 1912. In the mid-1990s, it was re-conceived as a temporary exhibition space for hundreds of artefacts from the Capitoline Museums, including the prized Santa Bibiana mosaic *(pictured)*. Taking up half of the floor of the Sala Caldai, the former boiler room, is this 4th-century AD mosaic, unearthed from the Horti Liciniani, a Roman patrician family's gardens, near today's Termini Station. The nearly complete mosaic depicts an elaborate hunting scene with life-size figures, which can be seen from either ground level or from a specially created viewing balcony 10 steps up.

In the museum space a marble statue and busts are juxtaposed in front of two 80-tonne diesel engines, while a rare pediment statue from the 1st-century Temple of Apollo Sosianus is displayed in the machine room. Before leaving, take a minute to admire the monumental grandeur of the machinery. Though not as creative as the Greeks, the Romans were always masters of technology.

Museo della Centrale Montemartini; Via Ostiense 106; tel: 06-574 8042; www.centralemontemartini.org; Tue–Sun 9am–7pm; charge; Metro B to Piramide; map B4

Get a taste of **1920s working-class Rome** in the backstreets of **Garbatella**

With an atmosphere that harks back to less hurried days, the neighbourhood of Garbatella gives visitors a snapshot of working-class Rome. Modelled after Sir Ebenezer Howard's Utopian Garden City projects in England, the enclave's foundation stone was placed by Victor Emmanuel III on 18 February, 1920.

In designing new housing for the city's burgeoning post-war labour force, Garbatella's architects came up with a capricious style known as *barocchetto,* a mix of Baroque, Renaissance and medieval.

The experiment was named La Borgata Giardino, after its garden courtyards, but residents soon began calling their new home Garbatella. According to locals, the name was taken from a tavern owner on the picturesque Via delle Chiese, who was said to be *garbata* – courteous and well mannered. Garbatella still retains its original soul and verve, and it is a frequent backdrop for Italian TV and film productions.

Begin your exploration of Garbatella with a cornetto at **Dar Moschino** (Piazza Benedetto Brin 5; tel: 06-513 9473; map C2). Afterwards, stretch your legs along the narrow streets and small piazzas, visiting Via A. Rubino, Piazza G. Sapeto, Via Angelo Orsucci or Piazza Ricoldo da Montecroce. These interconnected lanes and squares act as a frame to the pastel palazzi, connecting courtyards and whimsical building motifs.

Piazza Bartolomeo Romana, one of the most characteristic squares, is home to the **Cinema-Teatro Palladium** (*pictured,* tel: 06-5706 7779; www.teatro-palladium.it; map C2). Today the arts centre stages international music and dance performances, and participates in the prestigious multimedia RomaEuropa Festival.

Sip Negronis and dance the night away in the shard caves of **Testaccio's *discoteche***

Testaccio is the epicentre for Roman nightlife. Every style of *discoteca* from salsa and house to reggae and rock can be found in the small area encircling the ancient Monte Testaccio. For nine months of the year, from 11pm until the early hours of the morning, this neighbourhood overflows with music and people grooving to their own beats.

Tucked among the former stables and stalls of Via di Monte Testaccio and the storage houses of Via Galvani are Rome's favourite clubs. Here, it's easy to dance the night away unaware that the dance area is inside a series of man-made caves dug out of an ancient rubbish heap of amphora shards.

The music scene is anything but ancient, and hard-core clubbers will be able to work up a little sweat with their bump and grind. On Via di Monte Testaccio revellers can enjoy the notes of Latin American samba at **Caffè Latino** (96), techno and alternative rock at **Radio Londra** (65), and old-fashioned rock 'n' roll at **Coyote** (48b). To start the night club hopping, visit **Akab** (68; closed Sun–Mon), a long-term fixture of the Testaccio bar scene. Always lively, Akab hosts international DJs as well as live musicians. The underground dance floor, known as 'the Cave', can accommodate hundreds of girating bodies.

On Via Galvani the highbrow lounge lizard can choose from **Joia** (20) and **Ketumbar** (24), which combine VIP class with Italian sass. At Joia you can dine on classic Roman cuisine on the terrace, and groove with models on the dance floor. Ketumbar has a pan-Asian influenced menu and, more importantly, a very successful cocktail bar where

MONTE TESTACCIO

Monte Testaccio (Hill of Shards), from which the neighbourhood takes its name, is a 35m- (115ft-) high hill created from bits of broken pottery. The area was used from 140 BC to about AD 250 to unload supplies coming upriver to the capital. After the great jars (*amphorae*) of olive oil were decanted, they were flung onto the pile. The neighbourhood was a major gateway for food and goods until the mid-1970s. At the end of Via Galvani is the entrance to what was once the massive Mattatoio (slaughterhouse), which has been converted into the contemporary art museum MACRO Future (Piazza Orazio Giustiniani 4; tel: 06-6710 7040; www.macro.roma.museum; Tue–Sun 4pm–midnight; charge; map B6

former footballers sip Negronis. Further down the road and away from the hullabaloo is **Hulala** (Via dei Conciatori 7; C5), the posh lounge created by Parisian Stephane Rochet where coquette waitresses dress as cabaret girls from 19th-century Paris and waiters are costumed as mysterious Aladdins.

Throughout Testaccio, the evening party spills into the street regardless of the season or temperature. But most clubs close their doors from June to August, relocating to the beaches of Fregene and Ostia, or the banks of the Tiber, just below Castel Sant'Angelo. In general, clubs charge an entrance fee, which usually covers one drink along with your entry.

Monte Testaccio; map B5–B6

Compare a **scale model of the imperial city** with a Fascist view of the future at **EUR**

For an idea of what Ancient Rome actually looked like, head beyond the city walls to the Museum of Roman Civilisation in EUR. Housed in a Fascist-era palace is the *plastico*, a model of the imperial city in the 4th century. Based on the *Forma Urbis Romae*, a fragmentary map detailing the entire ancient city, this 1:250 scale model reproduces every nook and cranny. Visitors view from above the congested metropolis by walking around its perimeter. Recognisable sites include the Colosseum, the many imperial baths, the Forum, Trajan's Column and Markets, and the Pantheon.

In 59 sections, the labyrinthine rooms of the museum catalogue the entire history of Rome, from the 8th century BC to the beginnings of Christianity.

Planned in 1938, the EUR complex was intended to commemorate the 20th anniversary of Fascism in the 1942 Esposizione Universale di Roma (EUR), which was thwarted by World War II. Mussolini's neo-classical buildings recall imperial architecture, and were constructed in his favourite travertine marble, which had been Augustus Caesar's material of choice. It includes a Fascist remix of the Colosseum (square not round, pictured here), Trajan's Markets, the Pantheon and an Egyptian obelisk.

Museo della Civiltà Romana; Piazza G. Agnelli 10; tel: 060608; www.museociviltaromana.it; Tue–Sat 9am–2pm, Sun 9am–1.30pm; charge; Metro B to EUR Palasport; off map area, to the south

VN POPOLO DI POETI DI ARTISTI DI EROI
DI SANTI DI PENSATORI DI SCIENZIATI
DI NAVIGATORI DI TRASMIGRATORI

Hop on the train to **Ostia Antica**, Ancient Rome's extensive port city

For the cost of a metro ticket (€1) and a 20-minute ride, you can escape the city for a while and step back in time at the ancient port city of Ostia Antica.

Walking through picturesque and pine-tree lined ruins gives as good an insight into the everyday urban life of ancient Rome as the Forum, or even Pompeii. Founded in the 7th century BC, Ostia Antica at its height had 60,000 residents who occupied 49 hectares with multilevel apartments and houses, businesses (bakeries, mills, bars, shops), shrines, temples, baths, road and drainage systems, theatre, fountains and warehouses.

Decumanus Maximus, Ostia Antica's 2km east-west asphalt road, is lined with many sites. The theatre sits in front of a series of 50 or so office spaces by the Piazza della Corporazione, where mosaic pavements show ships and their cargoes of grain, olive oil, ivory and wine.

In the centre of Ostia is the Forum, dominated by the imposing Capitolium and antiquity's best-preserved and intact bath complex. Just down the road is the Temple to Mithras with a stairwell that leads to the underground slave chambers, and a sky-lit statue of Mithras.

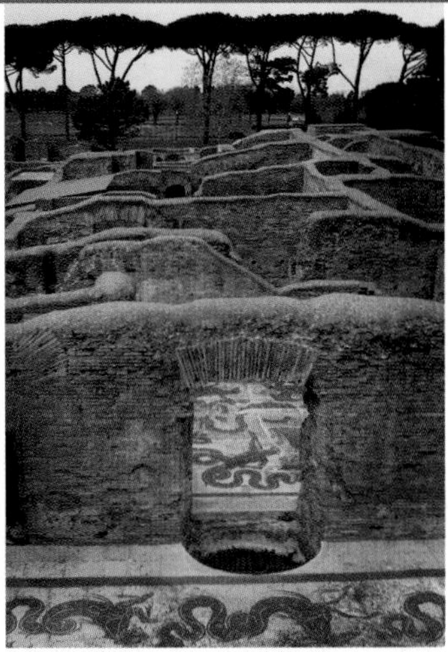

A 3rd-century AD white marble statue of Mithras slaying a bull, signed in Greek by Kritios of Athens, is one of the exhibits in the Museum of Ostia, which contains an impressive collection of sculpture found here and in nearby Portus. Imperial family statuary portraits, including impressive life-sized Emperors Trajan and Maxentius, dominate the museum.

Ostia Antica; Viale dei Romagnoli 717; tel: 06-5635 8099; www.ostia-antica.org; Tue–Sun 8.30am–6pm; charge; take Lido line to Porta San Paolo station; off map area, to the south

hotels

Even if Milan is the fashion capital par excellence, Rome can compete in cool hotels and old-school splendour. The peeling *pensione* of old has been supplanted by a wide choice of eclectic guesthouses. Diehard design junkies will find avant-garde interiors behind conventional facades. At the grander end of the scale, gracious, timeless hotels like Hotel de Russie retain their cachet. But for those not on an imperial budget there are plenty of bargain-priced B&Bs and family-run hotels. You can even go for the spiritual and stay in a convent, or live like a prince or princess in a 13th-century palace.

The area around Piazza Navona, the Pantheon and Campo de' Fiori offers the best introduction to the city, since you are right in its medieval heart and within easy reach of most main sights. However, there are relatively few hotels in the area, and these tend to be booked up early. The Aventine hill is quieter, although a little further out, as is the Prati neighbourhood around the Vatican. The Via Veneto district has a number of large hotels at the de luxe end of the scale. It is a convenient location, although the area is no longer the fashionable centre. Around Piazza di Spagna there is a more varied selection, while the Monteverde district on Gianicolo hill is dotted with turn-of-the-century villas, converted into welcoming guesthouses.

HOTEL PRICES
Price for an average double room in high season, including breakfast

€€€€ over €350
€€€ €180–350
€€ €100–180
€ under €100

The Lap of Luxury

Hotel de Russie
Tridente
Via del Babuino 9; tel: 06-328 881
www.rfhotels.com; map p.46 C5; €€€€

A favoured 19th-century haunt of the Russian imperial family, later frequented by Picasso and Jean Cocteau, this very grand hotel in Rome's most fashionable shopping area retains its celebrity appeal, with subtly decorated rooms featuring state-of-the-art technology, a tranquil garden, a superb restaurant and lavish spa.

Boscolo Exedra
Repubblica
Piazza della Repubblica 47; tel: 06-489 381; www.boscolohotels.com; map p.139 E4; €€€€

The opulent Exedra rolls out the best red carpet. The decor is neoclassical glamorous, with no-expense spared rooms where you can luxuriate in silky linens. Ask for one with views of the fountain. But what really sets this hotel apart from its top-notch competitors is the rooftop swimming pool.

Hotel Eden
Via Veneto
Via Ludovisi 49; tel: 06-478 121; www.edenroma.com; map p.123 E1; €€€€

Hemingway, Callas, Bergman and Fellini all sought this superbly positioned hotel on a hilltop near the Villa Borghese. The interior oozes luxury, with marble bathrooms, mahogany furniture and lustrous Italian fabrics and sheets. Views from balcony rooms, though not as majestic as some others, are still stunning.

Casa Manni

Centro Storico

Via di Pietra 70; tel: 06-9727 4787; www.casamanni.com; map p.25 H4; €€€€

Why dish out on a 5-star hotel when you can have a posh private penthouse? This apartment near the Pantheon is fabulously furnished with a terrace that's to die for. And you can have your personal concierge organise anything you desire, from a private dinner by a top chef to a tour of the sites with your very own archaeologist.

Residenza Napoleone III

Tridente

Largo Goldoni 56; tel: 347 733 7098; www.residenzanapoleone.com; map p.46 C3; €€€€

Rub shoulders with royalty in this luxurious boutique B&B owned by a real *principessa*. The Residenza Napoleone III, in the Palazzo Ruspoli near the boutique-lined Via dei Condotti, has three lavish rooms with sumptuous drapes, canopy beds, 16th-century tapestries and oil paintings.

Cavalieri Hilton

Vatican (Monte Mario)

Via Alberto Cadolo 101; tel: 06-35091; www.cavalieri-hilton.com; map p.68, C4 (off map area); €€€€

Sitting on Rome's highest hill, just north of the Vatican, the Cavalieri Hilton isn't particularly central, but a complimentary shuttle bus gets you there. Towering views of Rome, an Olympic-sized pool and a world-renowned restaurant, La Pergola *(p.75)*, make this an exclusive Roman retreat.

Cheap and Cheerful

Hotel Teatro di Pompeo
■ Centro Storico

Largo del Pallaro 8; tel: 06-683 0170; www.
hotelteatrodipompeo.it; map p.25 E2; €€

This family-run hotel, a stone's throw
from Campo de' Fiori, is built on top
of Pompey's Theatre where Julius
Caesar was assassinated. The walls of
the breakfast room were hewn from
the theatre's tufa stone, and bedrooms
are a cosy blend of cream decor and
terracotta-flagged floors. Excellent
value for such a central location.

Daphne Inn
■ Trevi

Via degli Avignonesi 10; tel: 06-8745 0086;
www.daphne-rome.com; map p.47 G3; €€

Guests looking for an intimate stay
with a personal touch will feel at
home at any one of the two Daphne
Inns. This elegantly designed
boutique hotel goes out of its way
for its guests by helping them plan
their trip, organise transport, make
restaurant reservations and provide a
mobile phone to use during their stay.

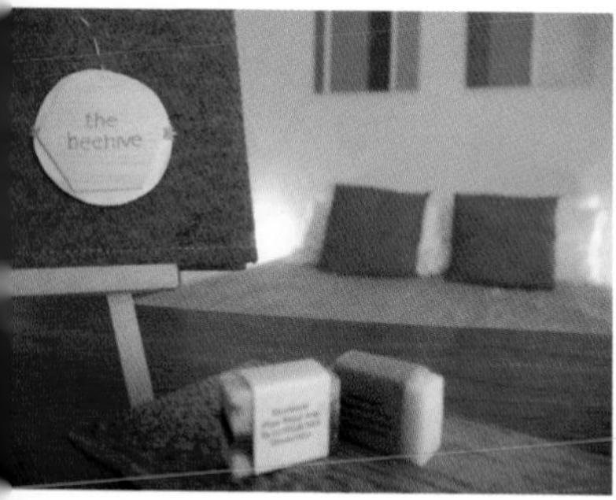

The Bee Hive
■ Repubblica

Via Marghera 8; tel: 06-4470 4553; www.
the-beehive.com; map p.139 G5; €

This trendy budget hotel/hostel
by Termini station, is an incredibly
cheap option. Established by a couple
from Los Angeles who wanted to
offer an 'alternative' escape from the
chaotic capital. With yoga classes, a
lovely garden, welcoming lounge and
vegetarian caffè, guests have plenty of
places to rest their tired feet.

Casa di Santa Brigida
■ Centro Storico

Piazza Farnese 96; tel: 06-6889 2497; www.
brigidine.org; map p.24 D2; €€

Overlooking the splendid Piazza
Farnese, the friendly sisters of Santa
Brigida run one of the nicest convents
in Rome. Conveniently close to the
Campo de' Fiori market and piazza,
Casa di Santa Brigida has a no-curfew
policy and will occasionally offer
papal audience tickets to guests. It
fills up fast.

Casa di Santa Francesca Romana
■ Trastevere

Via dei Vascellari 61; tel: 06-581 2125;
www.sfromana.it; map p.103 G2; €€

Hidden away from the core of
Trastevere, this monastery-turned-
hotel provides a tranquil stay in a
charming medieval neighbourhood.
A no-frills hotel with few amenities (a
TV room and a private reading room),
but there are plenty of eateries nearby
and the price can't be beaten.

Home from Home

Buona Notte Garibaldi
■ Trastevere
Via Garibaldi 83; tel: 06-5833 0733; www.
buonanottegaribaldi.com; map p.102 D3;
€€
Each guest room in this little B&B in
the heart of Trastevere has been given
its own stylish touch by the artist-
owner Luisa Lungo. Her artwork
which features in all the rooms, adds
to the colourful, warm and inviting
feel. She also has a private gallery, for
those who want a token of their stay.

Residenza Torre Colonna
■ Centro Storico
Via delle Tre Cannelle 18; tel: 06-6228 9543;
www.torrecolonna.com; map p.138 B3; €€€
Where else can you sink into a
rooftop jacuzzi with spectacular views
of Trajan's Market and the Vittoriano
monument? The Torre Colonna
guesthouse occupies a 13th-century
tower next to the Forum that belonged
to nobility. Contemporary and cosy,
it offers a reading room and internet
connection in all of its rooms.

Villa Spalletti Trivelli
■ Quirinale
Via Piacenza 4; tel: 06-4890 7934; www.
villaspalletti.it; map p138 C4; €€€€
Live like a noble for a day and escape to
the gardens of this Roman retreat just
minutes from the Trevi Fountain. Villa
Spalletti Trivelli maintains elegant
excellence without being uptight.
Furnishings are fancy but cosy. After
a long day's tourism, guests can stroll
in the garden, work out in the wellness
centre or have a massage at the spa.

Arco De Tolomei Guest House
■ Trastevere
Via dell'Arco de' Tolomei 27; tel: 06-5832
0819; www.bbarcodeitolomei.com; map
p.103 F2; €€
Among the cobblestone streets
of Trastevere is this gem of a
guesthouse. Just steps away from the
Tiber, it has the welcoming feeling
of staying in someone's home with
the added comforts of a small hotel.
Furniture includes family heirlooms
dating back two centuries.

Affordable Style

St George

Centro Storico

Via Giulia 62; tel: 06-686611; www.stgeorgehotel.it; map p.24 B4; €€€

True Roman splendour won't cost you a fortune at the St George. Upscale but not exorbitant, this sleek hotel is on one of the most romantic streets in Rome. Its decor is clean and cutting-edge. Its biggest conversation pieces are a sharply designed library, spa facilities and a *fabuloso* rooftop terrace bar *(p.35)*.

Relais Palazzo Taverna

Centro Storico

Via dei Gabrielli 92; tel: 06-2039 8064; www.relaispalazzotaverna.com; map p.24 D4; €€

Chic and cheap aren't easy to come by in the heart of the Centro Storico. Yet the Relais Palazzo Taverno just a skip and a jump from the magnificent Piazza Navona has a lot of sass and style at bargain rates. It isn't big (just 11 rooms) but is decorated in contemporary style with a funky floral flair.

Casa Howard Romana

Tridente and Trevi

Via Capo Le Case 18 and Via Sistina 149; tel: 06-6992 4555; www.casahoward.com; map p.47 F3; €€

Tucked away in a secluded palazzo is this stylish and delightfully eclectic 'home-from-home'. Its five themed bedrooms are decorated with great colours and sleek fabrics. And there's a Turkish hammam, too. A second Casa Howard at nearby Via Sistina offers more idiosyncratically chic rooms.

Historic Hotels

Hotel Sole al Pantheon

Centro Storico

Piazza della Rotonda 63; tel: 06-678 0441; www.hotelsolealpantheon.com; map p.25 F4; €€€

Opened in 1467, this is one of the world's oldest hotels. Opposite the portico of the Pantheon, it is comfortable and tastefully decorated without any fuss. Guests who want a bird's-eye view of the Pantheon should request a room that overlooks the piazza and its outdoor café scene.

Hotel Columbus

Vatican

Via della Conciliazione 33; tel: 06-686 5435; www.hotelcolumbus.net; map p.69 E2; €€

Not many people can say they have slept where the pope slept. But guests at the 15th-century home of the della Rovere family can. This High Renaissance palace was the residence of popes Sistus IV and Julius II, and is conveniently close to Piazza San Pietro. It has wooden beams and frescoed ceilings by Pinturicchio.

Hotel Hassler

Tridente

Piazza Trinità dei Monti 6; tel: 06-699 340; www.hotelhassler.com; map p.47 E3; €€€€

Here at the Hassler you'll find VIP views and a location that is simply the *crème de la crème* at the top of the Spanish Steps. Gwyneth Paltrow and Victoria Beckham are familiar faces, and the penthouse suite claims to have the largest terrace in Rome. Views from the Rooftop Restaurant where breakfast is served are priceless.

Hotel Locarno

Tridente

Via della Penna 22; tel: 06-361 0841; www.hotellocarno.it; map p.46 C5; €€

A classic Art Deco hotel in the heart of Rome that's been serving its guests since 1925. In its glory days in the 1950s, the Hotel Locarno was a classy watering hole for cinema buffs, actors and directors. One great perk: the hotel allows guests to borrow their bicycles free, an enjoyable way to see the sights.

Away from it All

Lord Byron

Villa Borghese

Via Giuseppe De Notaris 5; tel: 06-322 0404; www.lordbyronhotel.com; map p.122 D3; €€€

This small villa hotel, just north of Villa Borghese park in the well-heeled residential Parioli district gives guests first-class peace and tranquillity. Built into a former monastery, and garnished with marble and ancient motifs, it has the atmosphere of a vintage private club. Free shuttle into town.

Donna Camilla Savelli

Trastevere

Via Garibaldi 27; tel: 06-588 861; www.hoteldonnacamillasavelli.com; map p.102 D3; €€€

Guests at the Donna Camilla Savelli Hotel enjoy the true charm of Trastevere. Tucked away in a less crowded part of the district, it doesn't clash with night revellers. The rooms are modern and cosily furnished and there's a pleasant rooftop garden for guests to enjoy.

Aldrovandi Palace

Villa Borghese

Via Ulisse Aldrovandi 15; tel: 06-322 3993; www.aldrovandi.com; map p.123 E3; €€€€

This beautiful hotel near Villa Borghese has sumptuous rooms and sites, lush gardens, a spectacular outdoor pool and a Michelin-starred restaurant, Baby *(p.75)*. It's central enough to reach gems like the Galleria Borghese and the Spanish Steps on foot, though there's a complimentary car service into town.

Rooms with a View

Inn at the Forum

Colosseo

Via degli Ibernesi 30; tel: 06-6919 0970; www.theinnattheromanforum.com; map p.138 C2; €€

With Ancient Rome at your fingertips, views from the Inn at the Forum are unforgettable: the Colosseum, Forum, Campidoglio – everywhere you turn, you live, eat and breathe history. Walk past the entrance to check into the hotel and you'll uncover ruins over 2,000 years old.

Il Palazzetto

Tridente

Vicolo del Bottino 8; tel: 06-6993 4301; www.ilpalazzettoroma.com; map p.46 E4; €€€

From the rooftop restaurant of this small, stylish boutique hotel, there are spectacular views of Piazza di Spagna. Similar in style to its big brother, The Hassler, Il Palazzetto isn't as pretentious and its price tag is lower. It's also home to the International Wine Academy of Rome *(p.52)*.

Residenza Paolo VI

Vatican

Via Paolo VI 29; tel: 06-6813 4108; www.residenzapaolovi.com; map p.68 D2; €€–€€€

There's nothing more heavenly than the views of Piazza San Pietro that this former monastery enjoys. It lies on the grounds of 'official' Vatican property, and Pope Benedict XVI's portraits are everywhere. The guest rooms are comfortable and quiet. Breakfast on the rooftop terrace brings you close to St Peter's dome.

Locanda San Pancrazio

Gianicolo

Via di Porta San Pancrazio, 32/a; tel: 06-9727 3171; www.locandasanpancrazio.it; map p.102 D4; €€

In a green oasis near the Gianicolo hill, this hotel gives a sense of serenity from its rooftop terrace perched above Trastevere. Guests can take in the view while eating breakfast or over sunset cocktails. All rooms have comfortable, chic furnishings, Wi-fi internet access and satellite TV.

Hotel Albergo del Senato

Centro Storico

Piazza della Rotonda 73; tel: 06-678 4343; www.albergodelsenato.com; map p.25 G4; €€€

A room with a view of the Pantheon costs a little extra here, but check beforehand that it's a view worth having – it may be under the restorers' scaffolding. The staff at Hotel Senato are very accommodating when it comes to making guests cosy and comfortable, and families are especially well looked after.

Essentials

A

Airports and Arrival (see also Transport)

Travellers on scheduled flights land at the main airport, Aeroporto Leonardo da Vinci (tel: 06-65951) in Fiumicino, about 30km (18 miles) southwest of Rome. Some flights arrive at Ciampino airport (tel: 06-794 941), about 15km (9 miles) to the southeast. For more information, see www.adr.it.

From Fiumicino airport, trains run to Termini Station every 30 minutes until 11.40pm. There is also an infrequent late-night bus service. If you take a taxi, choose only a white one with a meter. Be prepared to pay a taxi fare of around €45–60 (depending on the time of day and how much luggage you have) to your hotel from Fiumicino; €10–20 from Termini or Ostiense. From Ciampino airport, a COTRAL bus runs twice hourly to the Anagnina metro station. Taxis are €25–40 into the city.

A private bus service runs frequently between Ciampino airport and the city in conjunction with Ryanair and easyJet flights (www.terravision.it). For a limousine service, for airport pick-up and tours of Rome, contact Airport Connection Services (tel: 06-338 3221; www.airportconnection.it).

Arrival by Train

If you are travelling from other parts of Italy or Europe, most trains arrive at the main Roman station, Termini. Like bus and metro tickets, train tickets must be validated at a yellow machine in the station before boarding. For routes, ticketing and reservations, see www.trenitalia.it.

Arrival by Bus

If you are travelling by bus both on national or international services, you are likely to arrive on Via Marsala near Termini or the bus terminal at Tiburtina Station.

Arrival by Car

Car travellers arriving in Rome from any direction first hit the Grande Raccordo Anulare (GRA), the ring motorway. The A1 (Autostrada del Sole) leads into the GRA from both north and south, as does the A24 from the east. If you arrive on the Via del Mare from the coast (Ostia), you can either join the GRA or continue straight into the city centre.

Various roads into the centre lead off the GRA. For the north, choose the exits Via Salaria, Via Flaminia or Via Nomentana. If heading for the Vatican area, follow the GRA to the west and take the Via Aurelia exit. If you're going south, take the Via Tuscolana, Via Appia Nuova, Via Pontina or the Via del Mare.

When leaving the GRA, follow the white signs to the road you want rather than the blue ones, which usually lead away from the centre. The city-centre sign is a black dot in the middle of a black circle on a white background.

Admission Fees

Museum admission fees vary greatly, but the major ones are €7–16. Most state or municipal museums offer free entrance to EU citizens under 18 or over 65. The entrance ticket to the Roman Forum can be used to visit the Colosseum. Entrance to the Pantheon and all basilicas and churches is free, as is entrance to the Vatican Museums on the last Sunday of the month (expect long queues). RomaPass, RomaPassPìu and Archaeology are tourist cultural cards that enable visitors to enjoy multiple museums and cultural sites at a discounted rate and within a certain time period. www.romapass.it and www.pierrici.it.

B

Business Hours

In general, shops open Mon 3.30–7.30pm, Tue–Sat 9am–1pm and 3.30–7.30pm. Many shops and restaurants close for two weeks in August. Churches typically open 7am–7pm with a three-hour lunch break (times vary). Banks open Mon–Fri 8.30am–1.30pm and 2.45–4pm; a few in the city centre also open Saturday morning. State and city museums are closed on Mondays. Museums, archaeological sites and other cultural institutions list precise closing times, but it is important to note that ticket sales stop and final entry is half an hour prior to the listed closing time. For a comprehensive listing of hours and contact information, visit 060608.it.

C

Climate

Rome enjoys sunny weather for an average of 10 months a year. The winters can be cold and rainy, but temperatures rarely drop below 4°C (40°F). In contrast, summers are long and hot, with an average of 20°C (68°F) from mid-May through to mid-October, with temperatures in July and August well above the European average high of 28°C (83°F). April, May, September and October are usually the best months to visit.

Crime

The main problem tourists experience in Rome is petty crime: pickpocketing and bag snatching, together with theft from parked cars. Leave money and valuables in a safe place, and keep an eye on your wallet. Be especially vigilant on crowded buses.

Report a theft (*furto*) to the police as soon as possible: you will need the police report for any insurance claim and to replace stolen documents. For information on the nearest police station call the Questura Centrale, Via San Vitale 15, tel: 06-468 611, or ask for the *questura più vicino*.

Customs

Visitors from EU countries are not obliged to declare goods imported into or exported from Italy if they are for personal use, up to the following limits: 800 cigarettes, 200 cigars or 1kg of tobacco; 10 litres of spirits (over 22 percent alcohol) or 20 litres of fortified wine (under 22 percent alcohol).

For US citizens, the duty-free allowance is 200 cigarettes, 50 cigars; 1 litre of spirits or 2 litres of wine; one 50g bottle of perfume and duty-free gifts to the value of US$200–800 depending on how often you travel.

D

Disabled Travellers

Rome is a difficult city for people with disabilities. However, things are improving, and the following have installed ramps and lifts: the Vatican Museums, Galleria Doria Pamphilj, Castel Sant'Angelo, Palazzo Venezia, St Peter's and Galleria Borghese.

For information on disabled access, contact Roma Per Tutti (tel: 06-5717 7094/800-810 810, www.romapertutti.it). Trambus (tel: 06-4695 4001; www.trambus.com) also offers a pick-up service for tourists with disabilities.

E

Electricity

Standard is 220 volts AC, 50 cycles. Sockets have either two or three round pins. For UK visitors, adaptors can be bought before you leave home, or at airports and stations. Travellers from the US will need a transformer.

Embassies and Consulates

Australia: Via Antonio Bosio 5; tel: 06-852 721; www.italy.embassy.gov.au
Canada: Via Zara 30; tel: 06-854 441; www.canada.it
Ireland: Piazza Campitelli 3; tel: 06-697 9121; www.ambasciata-irlanda.it
New Zealand: Via Zara 28; tel: 06-441 7171; www.nzembassy.com
South Africa: Via Tanaro 14; tel: 06-852 541; www.sudafrica.it
UK: Via XX Settembre 80a; tel: 06-4220 0001; www.britain.it
US: Via Veneto 119A; tel: 06-46741; www.usembassy.it

Emergency Numbers

Police 113, Carabinieri 112, Fire 115, Ambulance 118.

H

Health

EU residents are entitled to the same medical treatment as an Italian citizen. Visitors will need to obtain an EHIC card (www.ehic.org.uk) before they go.

US citizens are advised to take out private health insurance. Canadian citizens are covered by a reciprocal arrangement between the Italian and Canadian governments.

Chemists *(farmacie)*. These can easily be identified by their sign with a green cross on it. Farmacia della Stazione, Piazza dei Cinquecento 51 (corner of Via Cavour), tel: 06-488 0019, and Farmacia Piram Omeopatia, Via Nazionale 228, tel: 06-488 0754, are open 24 hours.

Emergencies. If you need emergency treatment, call 118 for an ambulance or to get information on the nearest hospital with an emergency department *(pronto soccorso)*.

Hospitals. The most central hospital is Ospedale Fatebenefratelli, Isola Tiberina, tel: 06-68371. If your child is sick, Ospedale Paediatric Bambino Gesù (Piazza Sant'Onofrio 4, tel: 06-68591) is a highly regarded paediatric hospital.

L

Left Luggage

You can leave your luggage at Termini Station for a daily fee per bag. Fiumicino Airport also has 24-hour left-luggage facilities in the international terminals.

Lost Property

For property lost on trains anywhere in Rome ask at the Termini Station's left-luggage office, located at the underground level (-1) near platform 24, open from 6am–midnight.

For property lost on public transport (except trains) contact the bus and tram network (ATAC) lost property office: 06-6769 3214; www.atac.roma.it; Mon, Fri 8.30am–1pm; Tue–Thur 3–5pm.

M

Maps

Free city maps are available from tourist offices *(p.186)*. Transport maps can be downloaded from the ATAC website (www.atac.roma.it), while more detailed transport maps (called Roma MetroBus) can be bought at any news-stand in the centre.

Media

Most important European dailies are available on the day of publication from street kiosks in the city centre, as is the *International Herald Tribune*.

The main Rome-based Italian newspapers are *La Repubblica* and *Il Messaggero*. Other Italian newspapers such as *Il Corriere della Sera* publish Rome editions with local news and entertainment listings.

The best weekly listings guide is *Roma C'è*, which comes out on Wednesday and is available from any news-stand. Listings are in Italian, but there is an abbreviated section in English. *Wanted in Rome* (www.wantedinrome.com), a fortnightly magazine in English, is another good source of listings information. *In Rome Now* (www.inromenow.com) is a weekly online magazine publishing information about the city.

Money

The unit of currency in Italy is the euro (€), which is divided into 100 cents. There are €5, 10, 20, 50, 100, 200 and 500 notes, coins worth €1 and €2, and 1, 2, 5, 10, 20 and 50 cent coins.

Changing money. You need your passport or identification card when changing money, which can be a slow operation. Not all banks will provide cash against a credit card, and some may refuse to cash traveller's cheques in certain currencies. On the whole, the larger banks (those with a national or international network) will be the best for tourist transactions.

Credit and debit cards. While major credit cards are accepted by most hotels, shops and restaurants, it's best to keep some cash on hand, as the card-reading machines are frequently out of order.

Cash machines (ATMs), called *bancomat*, can be found throughout central Rome, and are the easiest and generally the cheapest way of obtaining cash.

Tipping. Service is not included in a restaurant bill unless noted on the menu as *servizio*. It is customary to leave a modest tip, but nothing like the 10–15 percent common in other countries. Romans usually leave €1–5, but tourists are expected to be slightly more generous. When you take a taxi, just round the fare up to the nearest euro.

P

Post

Post offices are open Mon–Fri 8.30am–1pm; central post offices are generally open in the afternoon, too.

Stamps *(francobolli)* can be bought at many tobacconists *(tabacchi)*. Italian postboxes are red or yellow, but blue boxes specifically for foreign letters have been set up in the centre. Postboxes have two slots, *per la città* (for Rome) and *tutte le altre destinazioni* (everywhere else). The main post office is in Piazza San Silvestro, off Via del Corso (Mon–Sat 8am–7pm). The post office at Termini train station is open all day Mon–Sat.

Public Holidays

1 Jan – New Year's Day
6 Jan – Epiphany
1st Monday after Easter: Pasquetta (Little Easter)
25 Apr – Liberation Day
1 May – Labour Day
2 June – Founding of the Republic
29 June – Sts Peter and Paul Day (Rome only)
15 Aug – The Assumption of Mary
1 Nov – All Saints' Day
8 Dec – Immaculate Conception

25–26 Dec – Christmas and St Stephen's Day

Additional Roman Holidays:
21 April – Birth of Rome
29 June – Sts Peter and Paul's Day, Patron Saints of Rome

Holidays and Festivals

New Year's Eve is very big business in Rome: drinking, dancing, noisy midnight celebrations with firecrackers. It falls in the middle of a long holiday period that starts on Christmas Eve and lasts until Epiphany on 6 January. Starting 1 December, there is an annual Christmas Market in Piazza Navona. Easter is normally a three- or four-day holiday. On Good Friday there's a procession from the Palatine to the Colosseum (Via Crucis), during which the pope or a high-level cardinal walks the Stations of the Cross. On Easter Sunday, many people head for St Peter's Square at noon for the pope's traditional *Urbi et Orbi* blessing.

The city empties in August when many Romans go on their annual holiday. Shops and restaurants often close as early as 6 August to as late as the first week in September. For the past few years the city council has put on an incredible range of world-class outdoor concerts and other cultural events from June to September, and the city is less deserted than it used to be.

T

Telephones

Several companies provide public payphones that accept phonecards *(scheda telefonica)* only. You can buy cards in various denominations from *tabacchi* and from many news-stands. Some payphones accept credit cards, and many bars have coin-operated payphones. There are a number of inexpensive international phonecards available from news-stands, and there are also call centres where you can make your call and pay later.

For a number outside Italy, first dial 00 (the international access code), then the country code, the area code (omitting the initial 0, if applicable) and then the subscriber number. For international directory enquiries and operator-assisted national and international calls, tel: 892-412.

Landlines in Rome have an 06 area code which you must use whether calling from within Rome, from outside Rome or from abroad. Numbers in Rome have four to eight digits. Toll-free numbers start with 800.

Mobile phone numbers begin with 3, for example 338, 340, 333, 348, and cost a lot more.

Time Zones

Italy follows Central European Time (GMT+1). From the last Sunday in March to the last Sunday in September, clocks are advanced one hour (GMT+2).

Toilets

Bars are obliged by law to let you use their toilets. This doesn't mean that they will do so with good grace; if you don't spend any money at the bar first they may throw you a look. In many cases bar toilets are locked and you will need to ask for the key *(chiave)* at the till. There are now public pay toilets near most of the major sights and monuments.

Tourist Information

The following tourist information points or PIT *(punto informativo turistico)* are open daily 9.30am–7.30pm:
Piazza Pia (Castel Sant'Angelo); Piazza del Tempio della Pace (Via dei Fori Imperiali); Piazza delle Cinque Lune (Piazza Navona); Via Nazionale (Palazzo delle Esposizioni); Piazza Sonnino (Trastevere); Piazza San Giovanni in Laterano; Via dell'Olmata (Santa Maria Maggiore); Via Marco Minghetti (Trevi Fountain).

The city council offers a tourism information line (06 06 08; www.060608.it) with information in English available from 8am–10pm.

The Hotel Reservation Service (in Termini Station opposite platform 24, tel: 06-699 1000, www.hotelreservation.it; daily 7am–10pm) will make commission-free reservations for you.

There is also an information point in Termini Station, in front of platform 4. It opens daily 8am–9pm.

The Vatican Tourist Office (Ufficio Pellegrini e Turisti) is in Braccio Carlo Magno, Piazza San Pietro (to the left of the basilica), tel: 06-6988 1662 (Mon–Sat 8.30am–6.15pm).

Transport

Taxis. Meters in white taxis tend to start at around €3. After 10pm, on Sundays and for luggage there is a surcharge. You can order a radio taxi by phone (tel: 06-3570/06-6645), which start their meters upon your acceptance (the automated operator will give you an approximate wait time and prompt you to hang up the phone to accept). Fares are some of the highest in Europe, so be prepared to pay.

Buses and trams. Tobacco stores displaying a big 'T' sell metro-tram-bus tickets, without which you are not supposed to board a bus. Tickets are available as: a single ride €1, all-day pass €4, weekly €16, and monthly €30. Once on board, stamp your ticket in the machine. There's a fine if you're caught without a ticket or without having stamped it. City bus services are operated by ATAC (www.atac.roma.it).

The sightseeing Roma (www.roma.city-sightseeing.it) double-decker bus departs regularly from Via Marsala (Termini Station) and does a comprehensive tour of the city. The ticket is valid for a day and allows you to get on and off the bus as you please.

Metro. The metro is a skeletal system with only two lines, A and B, intersecting at Termini. It operates daily 5.30am–11.30pm (until 1.30am Friday–Saturday). A shuttle bus service (MA1 and MA2) substitutes the stops, but calculate time for traffic. From Piramide, there's a train to Ostia (Ostia Antica and beaches), a stop on the metro line B, and the 23 bus to Trastevere and the Vatican.

For more information and a handy route planner, visit www.atac.roma.it.

Trains. Should you want to leave the city by train, you might find Termini Station a frustrating experience with long queues at the enquiries and ticket desks in summer. You are likely to get better service from the city's travel agencies. Tickets must be stamped before boarding at one of the yellow machines in the station.

For information call 892021 or see www.trenitalia.com. Tickets can be bought online or by phone, and picked up (or bought directly) from one of the self-service machines at the station.

V

Visas

EU passport-holders do not require a visa, just a valid passport or ID card. Visitors from the US, Canada, Australia and New Zealand do not require visas for stays of up to three months; non-EU citizens need a full passport.

Nationals of most other countries do need a visa. This must be obtained in advance from the Italian Consulate.

W

Websites and Apps

Websites

- Information on cultural events: www.whatsoninrome.com or ww.inromenow.com
- Rome Tourism http://en.turismoroma.it/
- Roman museums: www.museiincomune.it
- Vatican Museums: www.vatican.va
- Ministry of Culture: www.beniculturali.it
- Cultural listings: www.060608.it
- Hotel Reservation Service: www.hotelreservation.it
- Rome airports: www.adr.it
- Bike Sharing: www.roma-n-bike.com
- Public Transport: www.atac.roma.it
- Trains: www.treniitalia.com

Smart Phone Apps

- Roma bus – bus, metro and tram listings
- AtacMobile – transport information
- iBike Rome – bike sharing information
- Word Reference: Italian–English dictionary
- Cool Gorilla's Talking Italian Phrasebook
- Rome Leonardo Da Vinci airport guide: airport information

Index

Insight Select Guide: Rome
Written by: Erica Firpo
Additional text by: Lynda Albertson, Nicole Arriaga
Edited by: Alexander Knights
Layout by: Ian Spick
Maps: James Macdonald
Picture Manager: Steven Lawrence
Series Editor: Cathy Muscat

Photography: 4 Corners 61, 164; Courtesy Acquamadre Spa 37; Nancy Aiello Tours 104; Alamy 30, 55, 94, 109, 115, 132, 167; courtesy the Beehive 174; Courtesy Open Colonna 149; Courtesy Camponeschi Caspar Van Andel 80; courtesy of Checchino dal 1887 162; Corbis 54, 78; Richard Cottonfield 113; courtesy Hotel Eden 172B; courtesy the Exedra 172M; Andrea Federici 81; Fotolia 140; Courtesy Freni e Frizioni 107; Courtesy The Goa Club 9B; Courtesy Fondazione MAXXI 10T, 134; Getty Images 36, 151, 159, 163; Courtesy the Hassler 170/171, 177T; Hilton Hotels 7T; Courtesy Hotel de Ruisse 7B, 63, 172T; Courtesy Casa Howard 176B; Istockphoto 27, 32, 38, 71, 89, 168; APA Britta Jaschinski 12B, 13, 16, 19, 49, 50/51, 70, 76, 79, 82, 86/87, 88, 90, 99, 105, 119, 124/125, 127, 130, 136, 145, 147, 152/153, 158, 160, 161, 165, 169, 175B, 176M; Alex Knights 60, 91; Courtesy La Perloga 73B; Leonardo 10B, 175T, 176T, 179; Courtesy the Lord Byron; Courtesy Casa Manni 73T; Mary Evans 53; Musacchio & Ianniello 17B, 135; Raffaele Nicolussi 118; Parco dei Principi 129; Pictures Colour Library3B, 12T, 14, 35, 40, 128, 154; courtesy Residenza Napoleone 111 173; Courtesy Rooftop Terrace Planetarium 75; Courtesy San Teodoro 96; APA Alessandro Santerelli 15, 97; Scala 31, 34, 39, 43, 77, 106, 114, 116, 117, 126, 142, 146, 148; Superstock 33; APA Susan Smart 2, 3T, 4/5, 6, 8, 9/T, 17T, 22, 26, 28/29, 42, 44, 48, 52, 57, 59, 62, 68, 72/73, 92/93, 100, 108, 110, 112, 120, 131, 143, 177B, 178B; Starwood Hotels 11; Roberto Ventre 64

First Edition 2010

Printed by CTPS-China

Contacting the Editors
We would appreciate it if readers would alert us to outdated information by writing to:
Apa Publications, PO Box 7910, London SE1 1WE, UK; email: insight@apaguide.co.uk

Distribution
Distributed in the UK and Ireland by:
GeoCenter International Ltd
Meridian House, Churchill Way West, Basingstoke, Hampshire RG21 6YR; tel: (44 1256) 817 987; email: sales@geocenter.co.uk
Distributed in the United States by:
Langenscheidt Publishers, Inc.
36-36 33rd Street 4th Floor, Long Island City, New York 11106; tel: (1 718) 784 0055; email: orders@langenscheidt.com
Distributed in Australia by:
Universal Publishers
1 Waterloo Road, Macquarie Park, NSW 2113; email: sales@universalpublishers.com.au
Distributed in New Zealand by:
Hema Maps New Zealand Ltd (HNZ)
Unit 2, 10 Cryers Road, East Tamaki, Auckland 2013; email: sales.hema@clear.net.nz
Worldwide distribution by:
Apa Publications GmbH & Co. Verlag KG
Singapore, 7030 Ang Mo Kio Ave 5, 08-65 Northstar @ AMK, Singapore 569880; tel: (65) 6570 1051; email: apasin@singnet.com.sg

Rome Metro / Suburban Rail

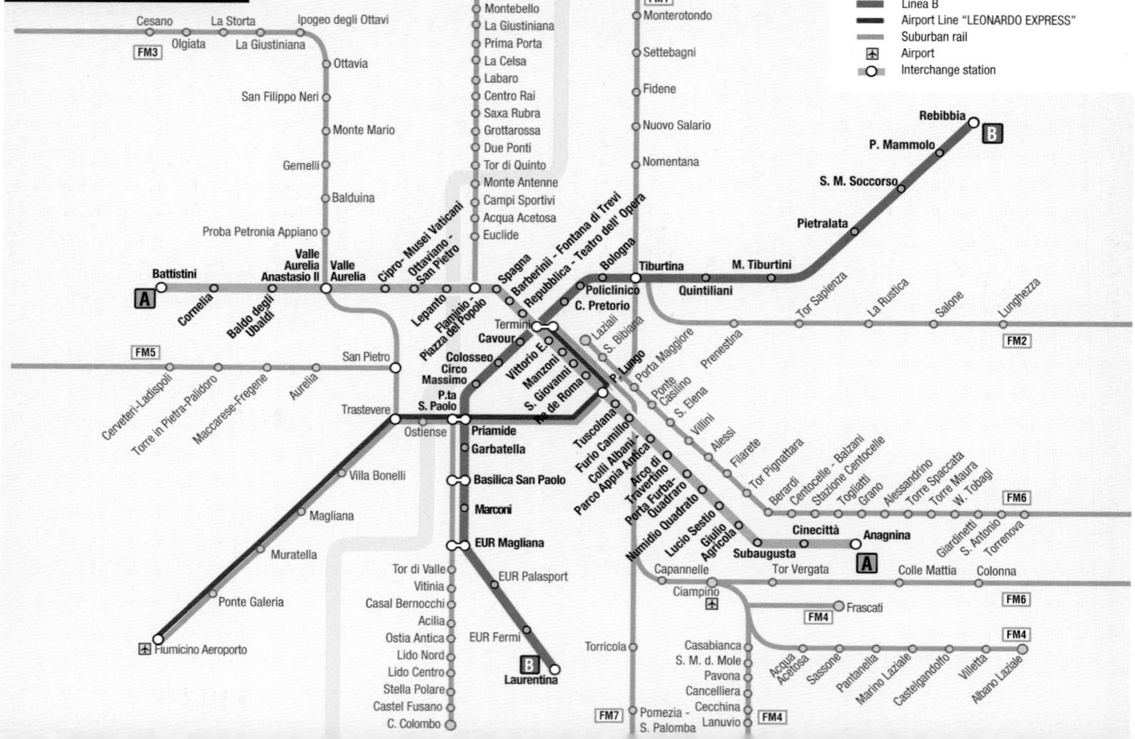